MICHENER
AND ME
A Memoir

MICHENER
AND ME
A Memoir

HERMAN SILVERMAN

RUNNING PRESS
PHILADELPHIA · LONDON

9 8 7 6 5 4 3 2 1

Library of Congress Cataloging-in-Publication Number 98-68459

ISBN 0-7624-0620-8

The excerpt from *The World Is My Home*, copyright © 1992 by James
A. Michener, is reprinted on pages 202–203 courtesy of Random House,
Inc., New York. The photographs following page 128 are reprinted with
permission of AP/Wide World (first and third pages); The Rodgers and
Hammerstein Organization (second page); Jack Rosen, New Hope, PA
(fifth and sixth page, bottom); *The Intelligencer Record*, Doylestown, PA
(seventh page, top left); Jeff Hurwitz, The James A. Michener Art
Museum, Doylestown, PA (seventh page, right); The James A. Michener
Art Museum Library (seventh page, bottom); and John Hoenstine,
New Hope, PA (eighth page). The photograph on the fourth page
is by Herman Silverman.

Jacket and interior design by William B. Jones

Typography: Palatino

This book may be ordered by mail from the publisher.
Please include $2.50 for postage and handling.
But try your bookstore first!

Running Press Book Publishers
125 South Twenty-second Street
Philadelphia, Pennsylvania 19103-4399

Visit us on the web!
www.runningpress.com

This book is for my wife, Ann;
our four daughters,
Jeffra S. Nandan, Leda S. Molly,
Binny S. Dilworth, and Jenny Silverman;
for our sons-in-law, Yash Nandan and
Michael Anthony Molly;
and our seven grandchildren,
Gita and Ravi Nandan, Eric and Griffin Molly,
and Vanessa, Ian, and Hannah Dilworth,
who give me great pleasure
and make life worthwhile.

Contents

Foreword

*I*t was a tiny corner of the world, but Bucks County, Pennsylvania, in the years immediately following World War II had the distinction of being very close to the heart of the theatrical world, and, like Marin County, California, was one of those counties in the nation known widely by name. An unspoiled, rural area only an hour and a half from New York City, it became almost overnight a glamorous place to be, especially New Hope, the village nestled beside the Delaware River that was home to the Bucks County Playhouse, one of America's most famous summer theaters.

George S. Kaufman, who provided Broadway with a hit play every season during the postwar years, wrote in a remodeled farmhouse in Bucks County, bringing his collaborators—Marc Connelly, Edna Ferber, Morris Ryskind—to work with him there. In nearby Solebury, Moss Hart wrote plays in his Bucks County farmhouse, and on one occasion— just for the hell of it, he said—he took over the role of Sheridan Whiteside, the leading character in *The Man Who Came to Dinner*, and played it for a week at the Bucks County Playhouse. Hart's theatrical friends infiltrated the audience and jeered and applauded when he substituted local names for characters in the play, an inside joke that filled the theater with New Yorkers every night of the run.

Refugees from the Algonquin Round Table, who hadn't been told there was a world outside Manhattan, came to Bucks County to search for their missing friends, liked what they saw, bought property, and settled there. Dorothy Parker and her husband, actor Alan Campbell, bought a house there, as did S. J. Perelman and his wife, Laura. Oscar Hammerstein II did much of his writing on his farm there, while Richard Rodgers settled for a while in the Stockton Inn just across the Delaware River from Bucks County. A few years after writing *The Good Earth*, Pearl S. Buck bought a home near Dublin in Bucks County, and Budd Schulberg, who had written the best-selling novel *What Makes Sammy Run*, moved into a historic old stone house near New Hope where he worked with Elia Kazan on the screenplay for *On The Waterfront*. Charles Addams, the *New Yorker* cartoonist, took a house near Bedminster.

The Bucks County crowd knew how to have fun, and they could even make fun of themselves, as they did in a hit play of the period called *George Washington Slept Here*, a comedy by Kaufman and Hart trashing the fashionable life of city refugees moving into farmhouses in a thinly disguised Bucks County. A song from the show *Farming* swept briefly across the land, a song that had "Lady Mendl climbing trees, Kit Cornell is shelling peas" and concluded that "Farming is so charming, they all say."

It was a great time—after the war years, people were eager to relax and enjoy themselves. Television was a new medium of entertainment, the theater was prosperous and bubbling with activity, and there was money that had accumulated during the war years when there was no place to spend it. On weekends, the yeasty town of New Hope filled with celebrities from New York, the Bucks County Playhouse was mobbed, and it was hard to nail down a table at any of the popular restaurants in either New Hope or Lambertville, across the river.

The lush landscape of Bucks County was also the setting for the remarkable five-decade friendship between James A. Michener and Herman Silverman. Michener acknowledged more than once that he had no closer friend than Herman Silverman.

The two men could not have been more different, even in appearance. Michener often resembled a distressed professor of Anglo-Saxon literature at a state-endowed college in South Dakota, while Silverman, cheerful and vigorous, always seemed ready to take on anything an antic and unpredictable world might offer. Michener, peering over his tortoise-shell glasses, gave the appearance of avuncular wisdom and reliability; Silverman, if not laid back, is unhurried, and certainly was the more versatile and personable of the two. Michener once wrote that "celebrity did not burst upon me in one mighty flash, blinding and disorienting me as it did to others," while Silverman did not become a celebrity at all. They differed in many respects, and perhaps this is why they complemented each other so well.

Theirs was a friendship born in the years before each achieved success, when Silverman was still planting trees and digging swimming pools on the way to national preeminence in the pool industry, while Michener was editing books—not his own—in New York, subsisting mostly on canned fruits, and spending country weekends in the spare room in the Silvermans' attic. They built their friendship brick by brick over the decades. Michener brought his second bride to Silverman's home to spend their wedding night; later, he and his third wife took dozens of trips with Annie and Herman Silverman. The Silvermans accompanied Michener to the opening night of *South Pacific*. When Michener ran for Congress, Silverman campaigned endlessly for him. When Michener was given the Presidential Medal of Freedom by President Gerald Ford, he took the Silvermans with him to the White House ceremony.

Their trust in one another was complete, but rarely discussed. Michener, Silverman has said, was so secretive that being friends was difficult. Nevertheless, the gregarious Silverman never thought to probe his friend's emotions or motivations—not even when Michener married for the third time, never having mentioned the woman or his intentions to the Silvermans, whom he'd seen weeks earlier.

Yet their friendship was based on more than their half-century of social give-and-take. They had in common the profound experience of growing up poor and fatherless, with responsibilities beyond their years. That experience shaped each man in different ways; those differences eventually played themselves out in the friendship, and knit the two men together in a bond they never put into words.

Silverman knew his father, and even after his father's death, when Silverman was nine years old, he never had reason to question his place in the tight constellation of his family. He grew up in Philadelphia, finding opportunity for after-school work as well as entertainment in that city's rich medley of working-class neighborhoods. Tall, with a thick cap of curly hair, Silverman greeted the world with an exuberant grin and an almost unbounded sense of the possibilities of life. The world, probably charmed by his optimism and persuaded by his energy and focus, grinned back.

In search of opportunity after high school, Silverman enrolled in the Farm School, now the Delaware Valley College, in Doylestown, in Bucks County, to take advantage of its free program in landscaping. The skills he learned there would provide the basis for his eventual success in the swimming pool industry, as the founder of Sylvan Pools. He also reacquainted himself, during that summer of 1940, with Ann Arbeter, a young woman he had known as a child in elementary school. They married in 1942, raised four delightful daughters, and have seven grandchildren.

I have known Herman Silverman for about fifty years—as long as I knew James Michener—and I believe him to be a guileless, totally honest man. He is the most secure individual I know, and if you understand that, you understand a lot about this relationship.

Michener, on the other hand, was raised in Doylestown by a desperately poor widow, with help from her two sisters. There were questions about the circumstances of Michener's birth, to the effect that he was the illegitimate son of the widow who reared him. In his 1984 book, *James A. Michener: A Biography*, author John P. Hayes reports that Michener was confronted with this rumor when he was about nineteen years old. But when he questioned his mother, she told him that she wasn't his birth mother, that she had taken him in as an infant. Michener accepted this and, ever afterward, claimed to be a foundling.

Their financial situation was so marginal that his mother, who took in laundry as well as other beleaguered children to make ends meet, sometimes had to send Michener to stay with an aunt—who, together with her husband, ran the county poorhouse. The young Michener passed time with the residents, absorbing their warnings against ending up as destitute as they. The experience drove him to excel, both in school and in sports, but it also left him with a lifelong fear of poverty.

"Jim told me he would never forget the sight of the wagon pulling up to the poorhouse, and some old couple would get off with just a few possessions, their belongings," Silverman recalls. "And they would be given a room. And one of the old men that Jim got to know told him, 'Jim, don't ever end up in the poorhouse like us.' I think that really stuck with him. He was always afraid, in the back of his mind, that he would end up in the poorhouse."

In his lifetime, Michener earned, through his writing and his investments, many times more than Silverman, though Silverman's success with Sylvan Pools made him, by any measure, a wealthy man. While Michener was protective of his millions, Silverman—a born entrepreneur—reveled not so much in having money, as in making it. If that meant putting some of it at risk, so be it.

"Making money is fun," Silverman says. "If it doesn't work out, it's still fun. I grew up poor, too. But I don't have that fear of being poor. It never bothers me. After I sold Sylvan Pools, I went into business for myself again—in fact, I'm still signing mortgages for $4 million for commercial properties. I think Jim respected me for that."

Of course, once he began to write, Michener was never financially impoverished. But there was always a vastly unoccupied space at the center of his personal life.

Other than his mother and two elderly aunts, he had no family. He married three times: the third time, in 1955, to Mari Sabusawa, a Japanese-American who, until her death three years before Michener's, provided him with constant companionship. Jim and Mari led a peripatetic life, traveling frequently and often moving, without benefit of belongings, to the location of whatever novel Michener was currently writing. They wanted no children, and had none.

But even after his third marriage, and certainly before, Michener lacked an intimate inner circle, a family to provide a welcoming hearth around which one could discuss both the important and unimportant matters of the day. There was no dinner table, none of the real warmth of acceptance that family usually provides.

So, when Silverman invited Michener—at their first meeting, in 1947—to spend weekends at his house, Michener accepted the invitation instantly.

The Silvermans' house was lively. Soon there were four daughters, each with friends constantly sleeping over, and there was a swimming pool which seemed to be occupied day and night. Sundays saw a large part of the neighborhood playing tennis or swimming there, sandwiches were consumed by the hundreds, and altogether, a passing stranger would have thought the Silverman home possessed a vital inner life that was noisy and chaotic but certainly a lot of fun.

It isn't easy to determine what effect inclusion in the Silverman family antics and traditions had on Michener at the time, but it was by no means trivial.

"I think he got a feeling of family, a feeling of stability and home. We were kind of an anchor for him," Ann Silverman says.

As for Silverman, he was initially intrigued by Michener's intellect. Michener had published several short stories in *The Saturday Evening Post*, but there was no hint when they met that Michener would become one of the world's best-read authors. Soon afterward, the stories were published in book form as *Tales of the South Pacific*, Michener was awarded the Pulitzer Prize, and Richard Rodgers and Oscar Hammerstein used the book as the basis for their Broadway musical sensation, *South Pacific*.

If Michener drew on the Silverman family's warmth and stability, Silverman took pleasure in the reflected sparkle of his friend's accomplishments and celebrity.

"I just liked to be around him," Silverman says. "He was a very good conversationalist. I never left him and felt that I had been bored or wasted my time.

"We frequently did not agree. But we enjoyed each other's company, and each other's outlook on life."

—*Caskie Stinnett*
   Former Editor, Holiday Magazine
   Wayne, Pennsylvania, 1995

Acknowledgments

*W*riting a book that covers a 50-year time span involves a great many people, and I would like to apologize in advance for any I might have omitted from these acknowledgments.

My first thanks—for this book and for most, if not all, of the significant happiness in my life—is to Ann, my wife of 56 years. She has been my inspiration and my support in all of my life's endeavors, and her memories of and insights into my relationship with Jim Michener have been invaluable. The loving family life she has given to me and to our four daughters, and, by extension, our sons-in-law and grandchildren, was important to Jim Michener, who had no extended family of his own.

Caskie Stinnett, a widely admired editor and a longtime friend who knew Jim and Ann and me so well, showed early faith in this project. His wife, Joan, worked closely with him on the Foreword and was very helpful.

Bruce Katsiff, Executive Director of the James A. Michener Art Museum, together with members of his staff, provided important assistance by verifying and researching key information about the museum and Jim and Mari Michener's participation in it.

I am extremely grateful to Blanche Schlessinger, my agent, for her enthusiasm and confidence in this book and for her many helpful suggestions. I am also grateful to my

editor, Nancy Steele, who believed in this book, edited the
final manuscript, and supported the project in many important ways.

Several of Jim's associates provided invaluable help. Sue
Dillon, his editor in Austin, Texas, edited my first draft to get
it ready for distribution to agents. John Kings, Jim's literary
assistant, generously helped check the accuracy of many
dates and facts. Even though they were still very busy with
Jim's personal and business affairs, everyone in Jim's Austin
office was most helpful.

Susan Caba edited a later version of my manuscript and
helped me focus it, and her professional journalistic expertise
was crucial in organizing its subject matter.

Daurelle Golden Harris was of great assistance in locating
photographs, and I also thank her for her help in reading my
collection of more than 400 letters to suggest which should
be considered for inclusion.

Jenny Pickett spent a great deal of time during her summer and holiday breaks from college in cataloging, filing, and
compiling an index of the letters.

I'd also like to thank my secretary, Sue Laudal, for her
work on this book, including long hours of typing and editing the lengthy manuscript at an early stage, which she did
with great skill. Her continuous involvement in this project,
and her almost complete memorization of the book and its
background materials, enabled her to oversee its organization as a whole.

Most important was the encouragement of Jim Michener,
who read an early version of the manuscript and who encouraged me to publish this book.

1. Recessional

*O*n Monday, October 6, 1997, I was working in my office when Jim Michener's longtime literary assistant, John Kings, called from Austin to say that Jim wanted to talk to me and my wife, Ann. John suggested that I call Jim in about an hour, after he woke from his afternoon nap.

I was immediately apprehensive. Jim was 90 years old, and very frail. Earlier that year I had flown to Texas to visit Jim, and when I left him, I didn't think he was going to live much longer. He was so weak and emaciated. His mind was still sharp and his speech was unimpaired, but I feared then that I wasn't going to see him alive again.

Nearly four years earlier Jim's kidneys had failed, and he was undergoing dialysis every Monday, Wednesday, and Friday. The three-hour treatments exhausted him, and he spent most of the rest of those afternoons sleeping. On Tuesdays and Thursdays he was able to devote his energy to the writing projects that still occupied his mind, but he spent much of his time in a large reclining chair, where he wrote, ate, and often slept.

The fact that Jim wanted to speak to us on the telephone only made me more uneasy. In the fifty years we'd known one another, we'd had many conversations in person lasting many hours and ranging across so many topics. But Jim disliked speaking on the telephone and seldom called anyone. When we did speak by phone, it was usually at my initiative, and it was usually a brief conversation.

I went home to make the call. Ann had just come home, and she took the other phone. Jim answered with a strong voice, and I started out by being cheery, telling him about the party our family had given Ann and me for our fifty-fifth wedding anniversary. Then I asked how he was feeling.

There was a pause.

"Herman, I think the end of the road has come, as it does for all people," Jim said. "The doctors have told me I have a terminal condition. And because some complications have set in, I have decided to stop my dialysis treatment."

We all knew what it meant. Without dialysis, he would die in just a few days.

Jim had explored many of the issues affecting the aging in his novel, *Recessional*, which had been published three years earlier, and recently he had been asked by a newspaper reporter if he had ever considered "pulling a Kevorkian"— finding someone to help him commit suicide.

"I don't have to pull a Kevorkian," Jim had replied. "All I have to do is pull the dialysis tubes."

Both Ann and I said how sorry we were that he was stopping treatment.

"It's a hard decision to make," Jim admitted.

As she always did during our phone conversations while Jim was ill, Ann asked the pertinent questions: "Jim, are they keeping you comfortable? Are you in pain?"

To our relief, he told us he was not in pain. And then,

for the first time in the five decades of our friendship, Jim told us what we had always taken for granted—that he loved us, and our daughters, and that we had been important in his life.

"I wish we were all together again," he said.

"We've had some wonderful times and I will miss them. . . . Goodnight."

After we hung up, I called John back to ask what had happened to prompt Jim's decision. John told me that Jim had developed gangrene in his left little toe and had had it amputated. His doctors wanted to add yet another day of dialysis treatment to his weekly schedule and to increase the length of the treatments from three hours to four. Jim had just recently undergone surgery to replace the dialysis catheter, because the old one had become clogged, causing an infection. These latest developments were enough to persuade him it was time to withdraw from treatment altogether.

Over the next ten days, we called often to check on Jim's condition. At one point, the news was bright—his kidneys were functioning on their own for the first time in three and a half years. He was also eating more, and had asked one of his assistants to bring him some "fried chicken, baked beans, mashed potatoes, and gravy—heavy on the mashed potatoes and gravy."

But the good news did not last. Late in the afternoon of Thursday, October 16, Jim died.

In preparation for his death, Jim had dictated a letter to his friends which was reprinted and distributed at his funeral service at the Westminster Presbyterian Church in Austin:

It is with a real sadness that I send you what looks
to be a final correspondence between us. The medicos
have left little doubt that this present illness is terminal. I approach this sad news with regret, but not with
any panic. I am surrounded by friends who support
me in these final moments with the same high spirit
they have displayed in the past. . . .

I reach the end of my life with almost daily phone
calls with beloved friends. Their spirits keep me alert
and their reminiscences keep me alive. A constant
hum of phone calls keeps me in touch with friends,
who bring me joy and a sense of continuing life.

I wish I could visit with each of you, but that would
be impossible. The phone calls, however, recall the
highlights of an exciting life. And they cascade back
now to remind me of the highlights: the running for
political office, and the drubbings we took there; the
victories we had in the theaters. I savor every memory,
as they parade past. What a full life they made. And
what a joy they bring me now; what a joy your recol-
lection of them gives me now. It is in this mood that
my final days are being passed. And I thank you all for
your thoughtfulness.

                              Fondly,
                              James A. Michener

Long before his death, I had done a lot of thinking about
my friendship with Jim, and about all the time Ann and I and
our four daughters had spent in his company. And I had
thought, too, of the question so many people asked over the

years, when they learned that he and I were friends: "What's Michener really like?"

Jim never thought of putting himself forward as a celebrity, or of publishing an autobiography or a book of his own letters. But often, when we were together in a small-town bookstore or at a roadside picnic stand and I would get it into my head to let the people there know that Jim Michener was right there among them, he would graciously respond to their attention. He understood that people admired him and were curious about him. He also knew I had kept the hundreds of letters we had written to each other across the years. On several occasions I discussed with Jim my idea of writing a book to chronicle our friendship and publish some of these letters, and he gave his consent to the project without any questions or restrictions.

There are sure to be biographies of Jim—the last time I saw him, he told me that at least three were in the works—but they will contain few of the incidents which I remember most vividly. What I want to share are the intimate, personal times we shared as friends.

Throughout the fifty years of our friendship, I knew Jim as a man of integrity, loyalty, and good humor. I don't mean to say that Jim didn't have his faults or failings. His own emotions were so tightly contained, and his focus on his work so intense, that he could be oblivious to the feelings of others. Many's the time I would remind him to acknowledge some honor or favor with a note; for example, he attended the wedding of only one of our daughters, and didn't respond to invitations to two others.

Even now, Ann and I have differing views on this aspect

of Jim. I looked at Jim as though he could do no wrong, and Ann looked at him as though he *could* do wrong—and did! I really had him on a high plane. Ann had a more pragmatic view: "Aloof," she calls him. We still have good-natured arguments about his personality.

After Jim died, Ann and I were remembering a weekend when we had a house filled with guests, many of them people Jim knew well. He came in, walked right into the den, turned on the television, and closed the door. "I don't think he even said hello to anyone," Ann recalled.

"He was very different from most people you would meet," I reminded her. "But he fit right in with the family—or did he?"

"Not really," she told me. "He wasn't the kind of person who walked in and became attached. But he was welcome and he was pleasant, and we didn't expect anything of him. There was that early period when Jim wasn't famous, when we were the only friends he had."

"That's because he was so shy," I said.

"He was *rude*!" Annie insisted.

"*Shy!*" I shot back.

"*Rude!*"

We burst out laughing. The truth is, Jim probably was a little of both. Ann likes to say that having Jim in the house was not like having another child, but more like having an adult who needed a home. She thought of him as tremendously vulnerable. He needed us.

Ann may be right about Jim having his faults, along with his strengths.

My memories of Jim are all sweet.

2. Radicals in Doylestown

I met Jim Michener on an icy January night in 1947, at a local meeting of a liberal-minded World War II veterans' group called the American Veterans Committee.

This organization was composed of young, idealistic veterans who were dissatisfied with the Veterans of Foreign Wars and the American Legion because they thought that those organizations glorified war. They believed that their new organization could be a vehicle to bring together liberal thinkers in the United States, and possibly to form a new political party to advance its social agenda. Franklin D. Roosevelt's son, James, served as its president. Despite the membership's high hopes, the organization didn't last more than a dozen years.

But before it disbanded, a small group of us met several times in a garage belonging to George Ermintrout, who lived in the village of Newtown in Bucks County, Pennsylvania, 30 miles north of Philadelphia. The handful of us from nearby Doylestown were probably the only liberals in our conservative community.

The night I met Jim was freezing. I was driving my 1935 Plymouth, which had no heat, and those of us in my car were bundled in lumber jackets or heavy car coats, with thick hats outfitted with flaps to keep our ears warm. I swung by to pick up an acquaintance of mine, Lester Trauch, an Army veteran who was a reporter for the *Intelligencer* in Doylestown. Les brought along a childhood friend, James Michener, a veteran of the U.S. Navy who had graduated from Doylestown High School the year before Les.

The rest of us couldn't help but notice Jim. He climbed into the car wearing a long black wool coat and a black fedora hat of a style I hadn't seen in ages. He was older than many of us—he was about to turn forty, and I was just twenty-seven—and his clothes and his rimless glasses, more typical of college professors than anyone any of us knew, set him apart not only in appearance but also, somehow, in intellect. Later we learned that he had taught English at two private schools in the area.

Just how different he was in intellect became apparent during the meeting. The discussion centered on a proposal before Congress, backed by the VFW and the American Legion, to give everyone who had served in the armed services a bonus of $500.

Jim was very vocal. He believed that to accept such a bonus would make us no better than mercenaries. He argued eloquently that we had gone to war because of our moral duty to defeat the totalitarian systems of the Germans and the Japanese, not for financial remuneration. I agreed—it seemed to me we were already getting pretty good bonuses from the government in the form of the G.I. Bill, with its free college education, low-rate home mortgages, and low-interest business loans. But there was argument back and forth that night in the garage. Eventually, Jim and I prevailed, and the twenty-

two of us at the meeting voted unanimously against the proposal (although later, Congress did approve the bonus).

I was intrigued by this newcomer. I arranged for Jim to sit
up front with me during the thirty-minute drive home. I
didn't know who he was, but I was interested in his ideas and
very much impressed with his debating skills. I asked where
he came from, and he told me he lived in the Village, in New
York City.

"Where do you stay when you come down to Bucks
County?" I asked.

"With my aunt," he said.

"Are you comfortable there?" I asked.

"Well," he replied, "I manage. I sleep on the couch in the
living room. It's a small house with only two bedrooms, and
my two aunts each occupy one."

Without hesitation, I offered an invitation. "My wife and I
have just built a house, and we have an unfinished attic. Stay
with us when you come to Bucks County."

Just as quickly, Jim accepted.

When I called the attic "unfinished," I really meant it. Ann
and I had just moved into our two-bedroom house on Old
Easton Road, and the income from my small landscaping
business didn't allow us the luxury of finishing the attic. The
walls weren't paneled, so the insulation showed, and the
wooden floor was bare. The room was outfitted with a single
bed, a chest of drawers, and a lamp; like most farmhouses in
those days, the only heat in the attic rose from the lower
floor. Nonetheless, Jim felt the sparse room was adequate.
We agreed that he would pay us two dollars a night. He was
then an editor for the Macmillan Publishing Company, and

wasn't making much money, but Ann and I realized that it was important for him not to feel he was getting something for nothing.

Jim's once-a-month visits to "Never Never Land"—the name of our little estate—soon became twice a month, and then it wasn't long before he was staying with us every weekend. He always arrived bearing food, the savories we craved from New York such as lox and bagels, as well as an ample supply of his own favorite—canned fruit. To the end of his life, Jim was a great fan of canned peaches, canned pears, and canned juices. Decades later, visiting him and his wife at their condominium in Florida, we found a kitchen stacked with cases of canned fruit.

Jim fit easily into our family's evening routine of eating dinner together in the small dining room. When we had guests, we simply expanded the table.

By then, the stories Jim had written while he was stationed in the South Pacific had been published in *The Saturday Evening Post* as short fiction and later in book form as *Tales of the South Pacific*. When we met, though, I hadn't heard of Jim's work, let alone read any of it. I can't say what prompted me to extend that spur-of-the-moment invitation the night I met Jim, except I could see that he was smart.

In the summertime during the late '40s, on most Saturdays our house was bustling late into the night with show-business people who were performing at the Bucks County Playhouse, which was going full tilt in nearby New Hope, or at the Music Circus, a summer theater just across the Delaware River in Lambertville, New Jersey. Ann and I would spread the table with cold cuts and snacks and open up the house. The theater crowd was drawn by the food, the fun, and our swimming pool, one of the few around at the time.

Bucks County was home then to many of New York's literary and theatrical bright lights—writers, musicians, composers, and artists. Oscar Hammerstein II, Pearl S. Buck, Budd Schulberg, George S. Kaufman, Moss Hart, and Paul Whiteman were all drawn by Bucks County's bucolic beauty, its reputation as an artists' haven, the easy drive from New York City, and the relatively low cost of a comfortable lifestyle. Beautiful old rambling homes, set on big farms, were reasonably priced. I understand that Oscar Hammerstein bought his spacious place in Doylestown Township for less than $50,000, and Moss Hart paid about $60,000 for his fifty acres in Solebury.

The big shots weren't frequent guests at our parties, but the "little shots" were. Then-aspiring actors such as Walter Matthau, Janis Paige, and George C. Scott would join the gatherings. Jim often showed up at these late-night parties. But few knew much about him, as he had not yet won the Pulitzer Prize.

One of our Bucks County neighbors was Dave Appel, a fine fellow and a prestigious book critic. Stocky, with a noticeable limp as a result of childhood polio, Appel was editor of *The Philadelphia Inquirer* book review section, as influential then as *The New York Times Book Review*.

I ran into Dave one day and mentioned Jim.

"There's a guy who comes to my place on weekends who's written a hell of a good book called *Tales of the South Pacific*," I told him. The novel had been published about six

months earlier, and I'd just finished reading it. Typically, Jim
had never mentioned the book to me. In all the years I knew
him, he would never talk about the books he was writing,
and rarely even touched on the ones he had finished. You
never knew where he was with a project.

Dave's reply floored me: "You can't tell this to anyone—
certainly not to him—but I'm on the Pulitzer Prize committee, and we're going to give it to Michener for that book.

"I'd like to meet him and see what he's like," Dave added.

I told him that Jim came every weekend, so all Dave had
to do was drop in around dinnertime. Sure enough, the next
Friday, Dave walked in as we were having dinner, and I introduced the critic to the writer. Each one knew who the other
was, but neither said a word about occupations. It was almost
funny; they just looked at each other as if they were afraid to
say anything. Maybe it was fear of letting something slip.

Dave finally spoke. "Do you have an agent?"

"No."

"Get one."

"Who?"

"Helen Strauss at the William Morris Agency."

With that, Dave got up and walked out. Not long afterward, it was announced that James Albert Michener had won
the Pulitzer Prize for fiction for *Tales of the South Pacific*.
Overjoyed at the news, we all celebrated. But Jim seemed to
take it very much in stride and never seemed excited—surprised perhaps, but as if it were nothing out of the ordinary.
He wasn't the kind of guy who showed much emotion about
things like that. I had already learned that his passions were
reserved mostly for ideas.

Jim did go to the William Morris Agency, and he did get Helen Strauss as his agent, a relationship that lasted almost thirty years, until Strauss retired. Jim stayed with William Morris throughout his career.

Many years later, in the early 1990s, when I was leading a campaign to raise money to expand the Michener Art Museum in Doylestown, I made an audacious phone call to the William Morris Agency. By then, Jim's agent was Owen Laster. I got Owen on the phone and I told him—only a bit tongue-in-cheek—"You know, you guys owe me a lot of money, and I want you to come across with a bunch of dough for the Michener Art Museum."

Surprised, Mr. Laster asked, "What do you mean?"

"Well, if it weren't for me you wouldn't have had Michener as a client. You guys have been profiting from Michener for years. You made a fortune, and now I want some of it back!" I related the tale of that conversation with Dave Appel some forty years earlier, and how Jim was referred to the agency at my dinner table.

Amused, Mr. Laster agreed with my reasoning and gave us some money—not as much as I had hoped, of course, but a pretty goodly amount.

In those early days, there wasn't a hint that Jim would one day be just as much at ease with potentates abroad as he was with us at home. When I first knew him, he didn't interact easily with people. We were often entertaining friends when he arrived, and it wasn't unusual for him to walk right on through the group and into the den, where he would open a magazine or a book. He did the same walk-through even when he knew the guests.

As for women, I'm sure a great many must have been interested in him, especially after he won the Pulitzer. But he didn't say much about any romances he might be having, and I'm not the kind of guy to ask questions. One week, though, he called before coming down to our house and asked if he could bring along Janis Paige, the beautiful and talented musical-comedy actress who had the leading role in the hit Broadway show *Pajama Game* opposite John Raitt. Jim and Janis slept in the attic. I don't know how they managed in a single bed, but somehow they did.

On another occasion, on the Fourth of July, 1948, Jim called and asked to be picked up at the Trenton railroad station.

Les Trauch and I met Jim's train. A tall, willowy blonde stepped down to the platform after Jim, but he didn't introduce her, so we had no idea they were together. Jim and Les and I walked out to the car and got in. So did the blonde. Jim still hadn't said anything to us about her, which wasn't too unusual for him—he was strange when it came to the social amenities.

Les finally turned to the woman. "Are you in the chorus of *Pajama Game*?"

Jim spoke: "If she were in *Pajama Game*, she wouldn't be in the chorus."

At last, confirmation that something was happening between these two!

Her name, we eventually learned, was Vange Nord. She and Jim stayed the weekend, and when the time came to drive them back to Trenton to catch the train, Jim had a request:

"I'm going off for about six weeks. I was wondering

whether Vange could come down and stay with you, and maybe you could look for some land. I'd like to build a house."

As usual, no details. But we agreed, and Vange showed up a couple of days later with several suitcases and settled in for six weeks, using our den with a pull-out bed as her bedroom.

She and I scoured Bucks County, looking for land. She planned to help design the house, and had good ideas about the kind of place she wanted. Jim seemed to have left everything up to her; he said he could live in a barn if he had to. And, as long as I knew him, he didn't seem to care much where he lived, so long as the rooms were large and comfortable, with lots of sunlight.

We found a piece of ground Vange liked, called "High Rocks," and bought it for about $2,000. But when he heard the news, Jim was very upset—he knew the high, rocky piece of land well. "That's where everybody is going to climb up the rocks and kill themselves. You'd better find me another piece of ground."

Jim was right about High Rocks. He quickly rid himself of the property by giving it to the Bucks County Parks Department. Even now, with high fences all around to thwart young, would-be mountain climbers, the rescue squad is called out each year to help someone down from the rocks or pick up those who have fallen.

Vange was greatly disappointed by Jim's reaction. Although she wasn't an architect, she envisioned a home like Frank Lloyd Wright's Fallingwater in Mill Run, Pennsylvania, with its dramatic placement directly over a tumble of boulders and water.

Three weeks later, we found another site in Bucks County, thirty-five acres of ground for a very reasonable $100 an acre near the village of Pipersville, in Tinicum Township, about ten miles from my own house in Doylestown. It was beautiful land, high, plentiful with dogwood and cedar trees, and offering extraordinary views. Before we could build, we had to bulldoze one narrow road up to the site and another one down. When Jim and Vange moved in, they had to buy a four-wheel-drive Jeep to maneuver the steep hill.

When we weren't looking for land, Vange passed most of her days drinking cup after cup of tea, smoking, and talking to Ann. I guess Ann and I knew that she and Jim were going to get married, but we didn't know the specifics. And there was certainly a surprise in store. One day, Vange got a phone call. When she was finished talking, she hung up and turned to us.

"Jim got his divorce—I'm going into the city so we can be married."

Divorce? We never even knew Jim had been married. And even after he married Vange, he never talked about his first wife; I didn't learn until decades later that he had been married for the first time in 1935, and that his first wife's name was Patti Koon.

The next morning, we dropped Vange at the Trenton train station. About seven that evening, Jim called: "Could you come pick us up again? Vange and I would like to spend our honeymoon in Bucks County."

Ann and I couldn't let a newlywed couple spend their wedding night on a single bed in an attic, so we slept on the couch that night and gave them our bed. But for many of the following weekends, Jim and Vange did sleep in the attic.

Soon enough, they decided it was time to begin building their house on the hill. We agreed that I would be Jim's general contractor, since he was traveling and couldn't be in Bucks County regularly to supervise the work. The house wouldn't be luxurious; Jim couldn't afford things like extra bathrooms and such, but we knew they could be added later, if he wished.

What Jim needed first was a mortgage. He had saved about $5,000, and we estimated the house would cost about $15,000. Jim asked the bank in Doylestown for a $10,000 mortgage, but the loan officer refused—the bank didn't lend money to writers, he told Jim. By then, Jim's financial situation had improved, and he had quit his job at Macmillan, but the bank considered Jim a poor risk, since he didn't have a nine-to-five job or a stable income.

I would have helped, but all of my money was tied up in my business. However, I did have one well-to-do friend, John Goldstein, a retired businessman. John let Jim have $10,000, at something like 4 percent interest. I understand that within a few years Jim paid off that mortgage, soon after the musical *South Pacific* became a smash hit and his career took off.

3. South Pacific

"*T*ell Jim I'm having a hard time with his book," Oscar Hammerstein II remarked during one of our regular Sunday visits in the spring of 1947.

During that time, I was meeting with the famed lyricist every week to discuss the landscape work my company was doing for him at his hilltop farm in Bucks County, and I had come to know him quite well. Hammerstein was in the early stages of adapting *Tales of the South Pacific* for the Broadway stage, and he knew that Jim had become a regular weekender at my home.

Several weeks later, Hammerstein had another message for me to pass along: Work on the play, he said, was coming along much better now that he had brought in the director Joshua Logan, an ex-Army officer, to help translate the book for Broadway. Of course, Hammerstein was also collaborating with composer Richard Rodgers.

Jim got an early look at the musical, and what he saw made him confident of its success. Normally not one to be effusive, he sent me, Les Trauch, and Dave Appel this undated letter, written in early 1949, before *South Pacific* opened, and while the songs and lyrics were still being finalized:

Dear Les and Herman and Dave,

Vange and I just had a most entrancing evening. By chance we stumbled upon a complete run through, without costumes, of the musical. Hammerstein and Rodgers have turned the original book into a master-piece of emotion, humor, and comment. There is no chorus, no set dancing. There is a big cast, and a very capable one. Pinza is terrific as the Frenchman, very warm and charming. Mary Martin is given everything to do, pathos, humor, dancing, broad comedy, chatter songs, and ballads. She'll be the talk of the town. A wonderful Negro woman is the Tonk, and she very nearly steals the show with two wonderful songs. Her daughter is unbelievably beautiful and ought to win the heart (or other extremities) of every man in the audience. Some dish! Luther Billis is a professional comedian who stops the show twice. Surprise of the evening was the naval captain, a 5-foot-1 brasshat who was perfect. Others were very good. The line of Navy nurses had real beauty. The sailors and G.I.s were appealing. Some cast!

The songs ought to be the talk of the town. Some Enchanting Evening should be a hit-parade item. Honey Talk is simply superb, a patter song combined with a dumb show. Dames will surely stop the show, a lusty chorus with delightful words sung by sixteen gobs. I'm in Love is a Mary Martin song that may or may not do well on records; as she sings it the audi-ence will howl, as they did tonight. I'm As Corny As Kansas in August should do well; I liked it more last time I heard it than tonight. <u>Younger Than Spring</u> is a terrific number as sung in the show; how good it will do alone, I don't know. There are at least six other damned good songs! And one will rouse you right out of your seat: <u>You've Got To Learn to Hate</u>. . . . I'll let you wait to hear that one yourself. You understand, we heard them tonight only with a piano, and they really wrenched the audience, believe me. And <u>Bali-ha'i</u> will be remembered for a long time to come. It's haunting.

The whole tenor of the show is superb. The pacing is a little slow right now, and twenty minutes have to be cut out. By then the show should really be a winner.

The thing that impressed me was the warmth and right-heartedness of the whole damned thing. This colored gal they have for Fo' Dolla' is terrific. She's really going to be the talk of the town. I doubt if Mary Martin ever had a better show. She has a chance to do everything she can do except drink a bottle of milk on her head. But Vange liked Pinza most of all. Boy, what a terrific voice, what a winsome cuss.

We are very bullish on this musical. It should run for two years. Herman, go ahead and put in the bathroom!

Regards,
Jim

Fred Waring was in the audience (along with a gang from Hollywood) and after the show he said to me, not knowing who I was, 'It's as good as *Oklahoma*'

Later he was introduced and said, 'Well, you know what I honestly think.' Let's hope he's right.

We had a chance to judge for ourselves on March 7, 1949. *South Pacific* was completed and about to open its out-of-town tryout at the Shubert Theater in New Haven, Connecticut. Jim, John Goldstein, and I took our wives to the tryout. We would have driven up to the theater early, but Jim had a speaking engagement at a hotel in Philadelphia and wouldn't be able to leave until early afternoon. Rather than risk getting caught in traffic, we decided to take the train up to New Haven.

The theater was old and beautiful, with chandeliers and fabric-covered walls. Even though it was small, as theaters go, it was large enough to accommodate the terrific, tropical-setting scenery.

You couldn't buy tickets for this kind of opening night because the producers "papered the house;" only important people in the theatrical community and friends and relatives of the cast were invited. There was a lot of excitement in the air that night. The audience was mostly theater people who had rushed up from New York to see what Rodgers and Hammerstein had cooked up for them this time. Though everyone was casually dressed, there was a lot of glamour in the theater that night. Our seats in the center of the tenth row were behind Danny Kaye and Ethel Merman.

The play lasted a lot longer than planned.

When Ezio Pinza, a first-rate opera singer who had never before participated in a Broadway show, sang "This Nearly Was Mine," the audience went crazy and wouldn't let the show continue until he sang an encore. The same thing happened when Mary Martin created a sensation by singing "I'm Gonna Wash That Man Right Outta My Hair" as she showered on stage and actually washed her hair! The audience demanded more.

The final curtain didn't fall until 12:30 in the morning.

The audience was silent for a moment, stunned by what it had just seen, then rose for a standing ovation. The applause and curtain calls must have lasted half an hour. People refused to leave the theater. When we were finally able to depart, we saw that Oscar Hammerstein had stationed himself at one exit and composer Richard Rodgers stood at another. "Did you like it? Did you like it?" they asked one person after another. These two marvelously talented men had just written one of the best musicals ever—and still weren't sure they had created a smash hit!

Jim's early assessment of the musical had been right on the money.

We were too late for the last train back to Philadelphia. Stranded at the train station, we looked at each other in dismay until someone asked, "Well, should we go to a hotel or just find someplace to sleep?" We opted to rough it on the long, hard benches at the station, trying to sleep for about five hours until the next train came through at 6 A.M.

The train station was empty except for a few bums also sleeping on the chairs and benches. We were starved, but there was no food around. The janitors who came through during the night were very noisy, swabbing the floors and cleaning up, so we didn't get much sleep. I wondered at the time what the public would think if they saw James A.

Michener, whose Pulitzer Prize-winning book had just been made into a smash play, stretched out on a bench in a broken-down railway station, just like the other bums who kept us company. By the time the train finally arrived we were all pretty groggy, and once on board we fell asleep immediately, not waking until the conductor announced our arrival in Philadelphia.

Jim, who rarely expressed much emotion, had already known that *South Pacific* was a great show, but he was overjoyed with that opening-night performance. He felt the Pulitzer had been important, but not nearly as important as having Rodgers and Hammerstein adapt two of the stories in his book, without a lot of revision, into a wonderful musical. He was delighted that their song "You've Got to Be Taught" had given the play depth during a period when racial issues were being hotly debated in this country. He also couldn't help but be pleased with his financial percentage in the play, tiny though it was.

When *South Pacific* opened on Broadway, Jim wasn't sure how many tickets he would be given, so I wrote to Oscar Hammerstein, who was in New York at the time, asking for two tickets for Ann and me. He responded in a note sent September 29, 1949, from 10 East 63rd Street:

> I suppose you know how scarce opening night seats are when a play gives its first performance in New York. I won't be able to meet your requisition from my own allotment, as I scarcely get enough seats to take care of my own friends. Jim Michener will be getting tickets for himself and his friends, and you will

have to get your tickets through him. I suggest that you tell him this, and that he can apply for whatever tickets he thinks he needs. These opening nights are really murder.

Jim did get tickets. He, Vange, Ann, and I saw the play together at the Majestic Theater. When the applause was finally over, we went to Sardi's to wait for the newspapers and the critics' responses. As we expected, *South Pacific* received great reviews.

One of them, though, really peeved us.

Several days after the opening, *The New Yorker* magazine's theater critic, Wolcott Gibbs, published his review, writing that he didn't know why Rodgers and Hammerstein gave book credit to James Michener since he didn't think the play bore any resemblance to Michener's book. Jim and Vange were at our home when Gibbs's review reached the doorstep. We were all pretty angry about his comment, and the more we talked about it, the angrier we got.

Finally, at about ten that evening, we decided to call Gibbs and tell him what a jerk he was. We reached him at home and complained. To our gratification, Gibbs apologized and explained that he had used as his reference a paperback edition of Jim's book which omitted the two stories upon which the musical was based—so much for the great *New Yorker*, which either couldn't afford, or wouldn't spend enough, to buy a hardcover edition of the book!

Despite the immediate success of *South Pacific*, none of us predicted just how successful the musical would become.

The New Haven opening had been on a Friday night. The

following Sunday, I had another of my regular meetings with Oscar Hammerstein at his Bucks County home.

"That's one hell of a play," I told him.

"It's nothing without Pinza," he said, indicating it was the marvelous voice of Ezio Pinza which made the musical a success.

Hammerstein was wrong. He had no idea of the musical's impact; the next year, it won the Pulitzer Prize for drama, and its first Broadway run continued for more than five years. Even now, more than fifty years later, it continues to be performed all around the world.

4. Vange

Vange Nord was an intriguing woman—tall, willowy, and Swedish-looking. She was very nice, very warm; in fact, warmer than Jim. She was easy to become friends with, and she was good for Jim at that time. While she lived with us, she spent a great deal of time with Ann, and later I got to know her well when we worked together building their house on the hill in Pipersville.

At one time she was an editor at a book publishing house. She wanted to be a writer, and I think she tried to compete with Jim—without very much success. When they were first married, she traveled a lot with him. And she put a lot of energy into building their house.

Vange designed the house. You could tell it wasn't designed by an architect, but it was a very pleasant house. It was a modernistic, one-story frame house with picture windows overlooking the valley. The living room floor was flagstone, and all the heat pipes were put under the floor to keep the floor warm. It was well laid out; there were two bedrooms, one bathroom, a big living room-dining room with a gigantic stone fireplace, a kitchen, and an office. Lumber was hard to get at that time, after the war, and I had to go into Philadelphia to pick up the window frames. But Jim and Vange managed to build the house for next to nothing; the land cost about $3,500, and the building cost about $15,000. In 1990, it was appraised at about $500,000.

Jim was away a lot, traveling in the Far East for *Holiday* and other magazines. Vange often went with him; they kept in touch with me by letter about the house, and I carried out their plans as their general contractor. They just said "do it," and that was it.

By 1949, the house was pretty much finished—Jim and Vange planned to do a lot of inside work themselves. We then concentrated on the landscaping; Jim wanted a lot of trees, with paths through the woods. He loved to spend his weekends there, walking with the two mutts he had adopted. Money from *South Pacific*, and the demand for his writing as a result of the play, meant that he had money to spend on trees (purchased from a local nursery owned by Dr. Stombaugh), as Jim indicated in this letter sent to me in the spring of 1949 from his apartment at 85 Charles Street in Greenwich Village:

Dear Herman,

Thanks for a lovely day! We enjoyed it immensely. Your mother was lots of fun, we thought . . . .

Here's what I'm proposing. You have some money of mine in [the] bank. Of this we were going to spend about $300 for trees etc. Let's do that (even though I said no on Saturday night. Changed my mind, like a woman.) Then add to it another $300 I'll get this week for various radio and speaking jobs. Actually, it'll be more than that, but I don't know what the commissions'll be. <u>More important</u>, I don't know exactly <u>when</u> I'll get payment. I should think by the end of the month.

So won't you please consider about $600 for the job? The money is assured, by April 10, I'd say. You can take Stombaugh into your confidence. But I'd like as many good firs, spruce, etc. as I can pick up. As you know, I'd rather have trees than furniture, and Vange agrees, wholeheartedly. So if the Stombaugh offer looks decent, let's capitalize on it. We'd also like the 12 other blue spruce from Perkasie.

Needless to say, Herman, Vange and I would both be unhappy if some of that $600 did not stick to your own delicately formed fingers. We want you to profit from the deal, but we also want to get the maximum number of cheap, big evergreens. It's your baby now.

As for the placement of the arbor vitae, Vange will tell you what the deal is, but in case she should not be available, we would like to have them some place in front, visible from the windows, but not obscuring the view. How about for masking that down-the-hill telephone pole? And we'd like a gang of them, and bunched together.

Greetings,
Jim

Some time later, politics in Washington played a role in the building of Jim's new home. Jim had a longtime friend, William ("Vit") Vitarelli, who had taught with him at the George School in Newtown. Vit is an ingenious guy, a sculptor who has great skill with his hands. When they were young, Vit and Jim once put together a puppet show and took it on tour through the country. Jim really enjoyed that; he didn't appear on stage, but he got an actor's kick out of performing through the puppets.

After World War II, Vit took a government job teaching school on the Pacific islands of Guam and Palau. He held the post for a number of years until the cold war of the 1950s. Then, unbelievably, he got caught in the hysteria of the infamous McCarthy era. Some unnamed person accused Vit of being a Communist, and he was fired. He had no money, no job, and a wife and five children to support.

Vit turned to Jim for help, and Jim responded at once, as he always did for friends. He told Vit to come to Bucks County and help build his house, and he loaned him money to return to the United States. Jim traveled to Washington, D.C., to testify that Vit wasn't a Communist or any kind of security risk. When that didn't work, he lobbied everyone he knew in Washington—publicly and behind the scenes—to get Vit reinstated.

It took three years and a lot of legal investigation, but finally it was determined that Vit was not a Communist and that he had been fired illegally. His job on Guam was restored, and he received a lot of back pay. Eventually he and his family retired in Hawaii.

During this period, Jim and Vange were out of the country quite a bit. Jim's work was very much in demand; the success of his book and of *South Pacific* made people curious about life in the Far East. Ann and I began receiving the first of what would turn out to be scores of his letters from around the world. (Not even Jim had perfect spelling or punctuation, and I've corrected his typographical errors and misspellings of names, but not his punctuation.)

It seemed that Jim always managed to get to an interesting place before anyone else knew it existed. Some of his letters read like contemporary news reports even today.

Bangkok, Siam
January 23, 1950

Dear Herman,

This is the place to visit! Such temples, such food, such fun, such girls. If Rodgers and Hammerstein can get even a portion of it into their next play it'll run forever. A really wonderful place. . . .

We've had a lot of excitement on our trip so far. In Jakarta, a traffic policeman, right where we were, shouted to a man on a motorcycle to stop. The man either didn't hear or didn't understand, so the cop raises his Sten gun—they all carry them—and klobbered the guy. The ambulance came around while we were still there to pick up the body. Nobody was much concerned and the cop didn't even leave his post. A friend told me, "Well, it does solve the traffic problem."

Vange is totally pessimistic about any long range prospects for the white man out here. We haven't been in a single spot where they didn't want him to get the hell out and where, in fact, they weren't helping him along. It's nationalism first and communism second, but the first so quickly becomes the second that it's hard to differentiate between the two.

As usual, I'm not so pessimistic and think that in the long run we can get back. . . but on their terms, brother, their terms. I've never really seen hate before this trip, and it's a bit disconcerting.

Mich

Sometimes it was Vange who wrote, as in this bit from an October, 1951, letter from the island of Java in Indonesia:

Dear Silvermans,

We drove into bandit territory yesterday. Beautiful country. Terraced tea gardens, rubber plantations and old volcanoes. Needless to add, we got the devil out before night fall, the bandit witching hour. As last Jan., the Army is ubiquitous. Makes one a bit nervous, the ready hand on the trigger of a Sten gun. Chinese here have had to observe curfew since the Red roundups of August. Consequently, dining with Chinese friends takes on aspects of a nursery supper and quick, what with the early hour. . . .

Jim and Vange would return to the United States for two or three months at most, then they'd be off again. Jim always left us itineraries so that he could be reached. He also kept in touch with my younger brother, Ira ("Izzy"), who was stationed overseas during the Korean conflict, which Jim was writing about for several magazines and newspapers.

In view of Jim's later remarriage, his letter from March, 1952, is interesting:

Dear Herman and Annie,

As you have probably seen in the public prints, I've been having one hell of a time in Korea. Those men are fighting a tremendous war on a shoe string. Don't let me hear any complaints against taxes!

The silly thing about my end of it is that I gave away the two stories for free, as a patriotic gesture and they were reproduced in most of the papers of the country. I feel like the prostitute who turned in a ten dollar bill at the bank, only to find it was counterfeit. "I've been raped!" she yelled. The amusing aspect is that the wire services in Tokyo got hell from Dave Appel's boss for releasing the stories at such a time as to fit the [Evening] Bulletin's schedule. "The only way you can square yourself with the Inquirer," said one man, "is to go out and get killed in time for the morning papers." Never happen!

Vange is in Paris, visiting her brother, and if I get through here in any decent time, I hope to join her there before we get back. If she gets home before I do, feed her lox.

I haven't heard from Izzy recently, but I've been in Korea. Your last letter asked if I thought Japanese girls would spoil him for an American wife. I doubt it. Wonderful as they are, they seem to get a man softened up for American marriage. Amazing fact: Of all the outfits that went really native in Japan, of all the

officers who took Japanese night-wives, of all the
enlisted men who had brown babies, of all the
divisions that screwed themselves right onto the
floorboards, which do you suppose was the cham-
pion? The California Division, where everyone is
supposed to hate Japs! By god, if you live to be 1,000
you can never understand racial tensions.

Just got word that Caskie Stinnett's rag bought a
powerful and poetic essay of mine, one of the best
things I've ever written. You tell Caskie I want it to get
the widest possible publicity because an enormous
number of people ought to read it. He can leave my
name off, if he wants.

Love to you all,
Jim

Jim loved all the travel, but I think it got to be too much
for Vange. After one of their trips to Japan, Jim told me that
she spent entire days in the officers' club, drinking. And when
they came home, she started saying she wanted to have a
child. I can only guess at whether Jim wanted children, but I
do know that Vange had been eager to become a mother.
They eventually turned to Pearl Buck for help in adopting
a child.

The writer Pearl S. Buck had lived in Bucks County since
before the war. She had won a Nobel Prize for literature and
was most famous for *The Good Earth*, her novel set in China.
She was very active in liberal social causes, and her speeches
often caused a stir among local conservative groups. Ann
and I came to know her while helping her raise money for

Welcome House, the adoption agency she founded to place abandoned Eurasian children with American parents. These children of American soldiers and Asian mothers were social outcasts in their homelands because of their mixed parentage.

In the early 1950s, Jim and Vange adopted an Asian-American baby and named him Mark. Vange seemed very happy. In fact, she and Jim later began proceedings to adopt a second boy from Welcome House, but a few months later he was returned to the orphanage.

On January 3, 1955, Vange filed for divorce. With attorney Ed Rome in Philadelphia representing her, she took Jim through a very rough divorce proceeding. She got a big settlement from Jim and moved with Mark to the Philadelphia area. We didn't see her after that, but we did have one more occasion to hear of her.

The divorce had been behind them for some time, and Jim had remarried, when Pearl Buck showed up at my home one day in 1956, saying that she needed to contact Jim as soon as possible.

Vange had called her: "I can't take care of Mark any more," she had said. "Come and get him."

Mark was four years old. Pearl Buck went and got him, then came to us to find Jim. She thought he could take the child.

Jim was in Hungary, reporting on the ill-fated revolution there and gathering material for his next novel, *The Bridge at Andau*. His new wife, Mari, was with him. I knew the best bet was to call the Press Club in Budapest and hope to reach someone who spoke English and who could find Jim for me.

I made the call and left a message to have Mr. James Michener telephone me as soon as possible. Within half an hour, Jim was on the phone.

He spoke with Pearl Buck and immediately decided it was not feasible for him to send for Mark. He didn't think it was practical for him to assume custody because he believed that his almost constant travels around the world would make it impossible for him to care for a child properly. I don't know what his subsequent discussions were with Mari, but Ann and I don't believe that either she or Jim was interested in having children.

Years later, in an interview with *The New York Times*, Jim said that he had asked that arrangements be made for Mark to stay with his elderly aunt until his return, but that something had happened, and instead Mark had been considered abandoned and had been placed with another family. Jim told *The Times* that he and Mari had felt that it was in Mark's best interest to avoid a custody dispute and to let him remain with his new adoptive parents.

I understand that Pearl Buck placed Mark in a home in the Midwest, where he was adopted by a loving family. I don't know whether Jim ever attempted to find out what happened to Mark. If he did, he never mentioned it.

5. Celebrity

*A*fter his divorce from Vange, and when he was in the country, Jim lived alone in his house on the hill near Pipersville. He would often drive the ten miles over to our house to spend the evening, and he and Ann and I would have dinner or go for a drive. These outings were the beginning of a tradition that lasted almost as long as our friendship.

In these early days, Ann and I were among Jim's still-small circle of friends, but after the success of *South Pacific*, his acquaintances grew to include most of New York's most prominent theater people.

Jim enjoyed these contacts, and I think he got almost as much pleasure from sharing them with his old friends as he did on his own behalf. In one letter from the early 1950s, Jim asked me to pass along a tidbit to his high school classmate, Les Trauch, a real theater buff:

> If you see Les, tell him I was astonished when I got to the dinner last night to find myself eating with Robert Sherwood, Sidney Kingsley, Madge Evans and Josh Logan. I thought about him all during the meal. He would have enjoyed the conversation even more

than I did; and I thought Sherwood was an excellent man. He really impressed me immensely.

Robert Sherwood and Sidney Kingsley were theatrical writers, Madge Evans was an actress, and Joshua Logan, of course, directed *South Pacific*.

One winter evening—as I recall, it was in 1955—Jim phoned. "I'd like you and Ann to go to New York with me tonight."

Jim could drive, but he never did on any of our outings; I was always behind the wheel.

"Jim, you must be nuts," I protested. "I have to go to work tomorrow morning. Who knows when we'll get back to Doylestown! And I'll probably get sleepy on the road."

But Jim wouldn't give up. "Well then, I'll get a driver. Put Ann on."

Ann took the phone.

"One of your favorite guys, Adlai Stevenson, is having a birthday party in New York," he told her—knowing that the liberal Democrat was one of Ann's heroes. "I'm invited. Why don't you and Herman come along?"

Of course, this was irresistible. About half an hour later, Jim showed up at Never Never Land with his car and a farm boy who lived close by to do the driving. It was nearly 10 P.M. by the time we arrived in the city and made our way to a fabulously beautiful apartment building along Central Park West. We took an elevator that opened directly into an apartment foyer, not a common hallway. I was impressed.

The apartment belonged to *New York Post* columnist Leonard Lyons, who knew everybody in show business. His nationally syndicated column about night life and the theater had made him as famous as the people he wrote about. Everyone loved Leonard Lyons because he always gave people in show business a favorable write-up.

When we walked in I had to blink. There was Marlene Dietrich talking to Herman Wouk, the author of *The Caine Mutiny*. Margaret Truman, Edward R. Murrow, Truman Capote, Leonard Bernstein, and another half-dozen show business notables were there as well. Everyone was casually dressed by New York standards. Sure enough, the guest of honor was Adlai Stevenson.

Ann and I were the only non-celebrities in the crowd, but we soon felt right at home because everyone we met was extremely friendly. Leonard Bernstein started to play the piano sitting backwards on the bench, with his hands behind his back. Truman Capote talked about a musical called *House of Flowers* that he and Harold Arlen had written; Arlen played the piano while Capote tried to sing the songs. I had a long conversation with Herman Wouk about *The Caine Mutiny*. I asked him where he had gotten the idea for the book, and he told me that an incident similar to the mutiny in the book had actually occurred.

It wasn't easy talking with Marlene Dietrich—she had quite a heavy accent—but she was down-to-earth. Later in the evening, the Lyons' two children were running all over the place, and when Mrs. Lyons tried to put them to bed, they refused until Marlene Dietrich said, "C'mon. I'll put them to bed."

Of course, we made it a point to talk with Adlai Stevenson, who had unsuccessfully run for President against Eisenhower. When he learned that Ann and I were practically the only Democrats in Bucks County, he laughed and said, "That's great. Now we have a foothold. We can build on that."

The evening was exhilarating. Jim and Ann and I managed to get home by four in the morning, after a truly memorable night.

Our hobnobbing with celebrities didn't end there. Occasionally Ann and I would go to New York to see a show, and often we wound up at Sardi's for a bite to eat with another friend of ours, Max Eisen, a press agent well known in New York in those days. Max liked to go to Sardi's to see clients. One night, several years after Stevenson's birthday party, Ann and I were having dinner at Sardi's with Max when Leonard Lyons spied him and came over to our table. Max attempted an introduction: "Leonard, I want you to meet my friends."

Lyons looked at Ann and me and said, "Of course, these are the Silvermans from Bucks County." Extraordinary: Lyons had met us just that one evening in his apartment years before, yet he remembered our names and faces and where we came from. I guess that's what helped make him a great columnist.

Early in my friendship with Jim, I came to understand that he had strong opinions about success—especially financial success. One day, a call came from Jim at his home.

"Herman, I want to go into New York and pick up some radio stuff. Why don't you come along?" He was installing a state-of-the-art stereo system in his home; Jim loved music, and listened to it while he was working. He had a large collection of opera recordings and once said that he tried to listen to opera every day. He also collected music from the regions and time periods he was writing about; for example, when he was writing *Mexico*, he played traditional Mexican ballads and *mariachi* music.

Since this was a daytime call, I agreed right away to join him. I wound up some business and we headed into Manhattan about one in the afternoon.

Jim suggested we stop at Toots Shor's, a famous bar and restaurant patronized by sports and theater celebrities. The place was just about empty when we walked in. Toots Shor himself was behind the bar, and he called out "Hiya, Jim, you bum"—which surprised me, because although Jim didn't drink, he was obviously a regular there.

In the dining room we saw Leonard Lyons sitting with Jackie Gleason, who was at the peak of his popularity with his hit TV show, *The Honeymooners*. Gleason had just signed a multi-million-dollar deal to renew his contract for the show, which was creating a big stir in the entertainment world.

We joined Lyons at his table, but for some reason he didn't introduce us. The silence was awkward. Gleason looked at us, we looked at him, and nobody said a word. Finally Gleason asked, "Are you guys with the Buick people?" The Buick division of General Motors was Gleason's big sponsor.

Jim stared at Gleason and answered, "My friend here drives a Buick."

"What do you think of my contract?"

Jim paused and said, "Well, I wouldn't think a heck of a lot of it unless you spread around a good portion of it."

Gleason retorted, "Spread it around? Hell, Art Carney is

getting his dollars, Audrey Meadows is getting hers. I spread it around pretty good." Jim got up and walked out. I followed. We had only been in Shor's about five minutes.

I don't believe Gleason ever knew who was sitting at the table with him, or that he ever understood what Jim was talking about.

As Jim's circle of friends widened, it seemed that he knew almost everybody of any importance. He was on the board of the Voice of America, and he served on the U.S. Postal Service Stamp Board with the people who decide what or who is to be depicted on postage stamps. He was an avid stamp collector, and when New York City was celebrating the 100th anniversary of the Brooklyn Bridge, Norman Mailer wrote to ask, "Very Big Bull Moose Michener—can you get a stamp made to celebrate the Brooklyn Bridge's anniversary?" (I believe Mailer called Jim "Big Bull Moose" because at one time Jim was quite robust.)

In 1975, President Gerald Ford appointed Jim to the advisory committee on the American bicentennial. Two years later, Jim phoned one day to say that he was to receive America's highest civilian honor: the President's Medal of Freedom. And he wanted Ann and me to be his guests at the White House ceremony, together with Les Trauch, his oldest friend.

The ceremony was set for January 10, 1977, in the closing days of President Ford's administration. By then Jim had been remarried for many years, to Mari Sabusawa, and Ann and Les and I rode the train down to Washington to meet Jim and Mari the day before the ceremony. After checking into the Hay-Adams Hotel, we all celebrated over dinner.

In the morning, Jim and Mari departed for the White House in style in a limousine, and the rest of us caught a cab. After showing two passes—one to enter the front gates, and another to enter the White House—we were admitted and ushered into the East Room. Press photographers and TV cameras were there to record the ceremony that followed: among the dazzling group of artists, writers, scientists, statesmen, and other American heroes honored that day were General Omar Bradley, Bruce Catton, Ariel and Will Durant, Arthur Fiedler, Lady Bird Johnson, and James D. Watson.

After opening remarks in which he praised the energy and imagination of the honorees, President Ford read a citation and presented the medal to each one. Beginning with union organizer I. W. Abel, the President made the presentations in alphabetical order, and after reading the citation for playwright Archibald MacLeish, he read the name "James A. Michener," followed by this citation:

"Author, teacher and popular historian, James Michener has entranced a generation with his compelling essays and novels. From *Tales of the South Pacific* to *Centennial*, the prolific writings of this master storyteller have expanded the knowledge and enriched the lives of millions." Then he presented the Medal of Freedom to Jim and hung it around his neck on a long, handsome ribbon.

Next came presentations to Vice-President Nelson A. Rockefeller and to Jarvis Rockwell, who was representing his father, Norman Rockwell. Needless to say, Jim's old friends were proud to see him in such good company.

In later years, from 1979 to 1973, Jim served on the advisory council to the National Air and Space Administration

(NASA). He attended its meetings several times a year, and he was always invited to watch when rockets were launched.

Once, while he was writing *Chesapeake*, Jim phoned from Maryland to ask, "Why don't you and Ann come down to the Eastern Shore and spend the night? We'll take a ride down to Chincoteague Island."

At that time he was living in St. Michaels, Maryland, to work on his book. Chincoteague, the island wildlife preserve off the coast of Virginia, is known for its beautiful beaches and for the yearly roundup of wild horses on the island, and NASA had invited Jim to visit its nearby space flight center on Wallops Island.

Ann and I drove to St. Michaels and stayed overnight at the Micheners' home, just a few feet from the waters of the Chesapeake Bay. The next morning we drove two hours south of the Maryland border to the tremendous NASA airfield with its huge aircraft. We saw rooms outfitted with all sorts of sophisticated equipment for various airborne tests, and the operations room where technicians kept track of rocket launches and moon landings. I think Jim already knew, at least in the back of his mind, that he would write the book about space exploration that was eventually published under the title *Space*.

On the return trip to St. Michaels, I took full advantage of traveling with a famous writer. During our excursions we liked to tour small towns, and Jim always insisted on poking his head into the local library. He wanted to know "What kind of library do they have? Is it big? Small? New? Old? What's the librarian like?"

We stopped in one small town in Maryland, asked where

the library was, and were pointed toward an old one-room schoolhouse. Inside were about a dozen women making potpourri to raise money for the library.

I walked over to one of the women and said, as I often liked to do, "That's James Michener over there."

She turned and gasped, "My God!" The other women became so excited—they ran over and began talking all at once, shaking Jim's hand and asking if he would please go to meet the mayor. They literally dragged him out of the library and up the street to the little town hall, where Jim met the mayor and everybody made a big fuss.

Another day, we were out on a pleasure ride and stopped at a bookstore where I again did a bit of name-dropping. While Jim was looking over the bookstalls, I went over to the young woman at the desk and said, "You see that man over there? That's James A. Michener, the writer."

"It doesn't look like him," she sniffed.

I went over to the bookshelf, selected one of Jim's books with a photograph of him on the back cover, and showed it to her. That got her moving. She scurried all over, picking up all the Michener books she could lay her hands on, hardcover and paperback, and Jim sat down and signed them all.

Jim would never have introduced himself. But I knew he enjoyed the recognition, just as I got a kick out of causing a stir by pointing him out during all the years of our friendship. It was my way of sharing my famous friend with others, just as he shared his glamorous contacts with Ann and me.

6. Jim and Mari

Jim was a very private person.

I never asked him anything of a personal nature; I figured if he wanted me to know, he'd tell me. Most of what I know about his early life, I learned from his novel, *The Fires of Spring*, a fictional chronicle, at least in part, of his childhood in Doylestown. His reticence to communicate ranged from minor matters—his scheduled appearances on television news shows, which we would have loved to watch—to the most meaningful. Only once did he and I talk about what was possibly the defining feature of our young lives, growing up without our fathers.

So after his divorce from Vange, I guess I shouldn't have been surprised to pick up a copy of LIFE magazine in my hotel room in Rome in the fall of 1955 and see photographs of Jim being married to a Japanese-American woman in Chicago! Three weeks earlier, Jim had driven Ann and me to the airport and said not a word about his intention to get married. We hadn't even known of the *existence* of Mari Yoriko Sabusawa.

Later we learned that Jim had met Mari in Chicago some time earlier. When he visited Chicago, Jim was researching an article for LIFE on marriages between American men and Japanese women. Mari (who was single, but who worked with Japanese brides who were new to America) was invited to a luncheon held on Jim's behalf with other experts on the topic. Afterward, Jim left the country for several months, but Mari must have made quite an impression on him. They were married at the end of his second trip to Chicago, on October 23, 1955.

We didn't get a chance to meet Mari for several more months. After Jim and Mari were married, they left on one of Jim's extended journeys. He usually left me an itinerary, and the one for this trip shows the two of them heading for Australia in November, moving on to Bombay, then to Bangkok, Singapore, Hong Kong, and finally to Japan before arriving in Hawaii. Mari was Nisei, born in America of Japanese parents, but she had never been to Japan.

On November 25, Jim wrote from Australia, the first leg of their trip, making it clear he was very happy:

> My lady has been a sensation in Australia, where they hate the Japanese, and with some reason. She has wonderful good sense, a fine timing in her humor and an enormous energy. She has been on the front pages of the Australian press for about two weeks and seems always to have exactly the right thing to say. . . . She is a load of fun, and I am sure you and your gang will love her. I know I do.

A few weeks later, we received another letter from Australia, this one addressed to Jim's two aunts and copied, as Jim often did, to me, with a note to pass it along to Lester Trauch. In it, Jim introduced Mari:

In The Heart of Australia
December 12, 1955

Dear Aunt Hannah and Aunt Laura,

A good many people have been inquiring as to what kind of person my wife, Mari, is, and we feel as if our hurried departure for Asia robbed our friends of their natural interest in our marriage. I should therefore like to comment briefly on your new neighbor, at Christmas time.

Mari Yoriko Sabusawa was born July 10, 1920 in Las Animas, Colorado, where her father and mother had a melon ranch on the edge of the great drylands of the west. Both of her parents were born in Japan and had come to the U.S. in the early 1900's. Her sister was born in Japan and her brother in Denver. Her father is now dead, but her mother lives in a small town in Colorado. A friend of mine has called Mrs. Sabusawa the perfect mother-in-law: "She lives 2,000 miles away and can't speak your language." I am, however, learning Japanese.

When Mari was 15, her family moved to Southern Calif. After Pearl Harbor, she with 110,000 other persons of Japanese ancestry and citizen and non-citizen alike were evacuated from the West Coast. She spent some time as an internee at the Santa Anita Race Track, where she occupied the stable once made famous by Equipoise.

After four months (there were 20,000 evacuees there) Mari was moved to a relocation center near

Granada, Colorado, where outside of the camp lived several of the friends with whom she grew up in Colorado, while she was kept behind barbed wire in "protective custody."

Quickly, she was among the first selected on indefinite leave to see if American campuses and their communities would accept Japanese relocatees. She entered Antioch College as a junior and had two delightful years there without incident. Arthur E. Morgan one time head of TVA and 10 years president of Antioch did much to pave the way for her coming to Antioch. She was given an Antioch scholarship and was sponsored by the American Baptist Home Mission Society, whose guiding spirit now lives in Ringoes, N.J. Mari refers to Dr. Thomas as "my adopted father."

She graduated from Antioch (in the class ahead of Pearl Buck's daughter) with good grades in political science and international relations. During one of her cooperative jobs required at Antioch, she worked as an analyst for Foreign Broadcast Intelligence Service in the Analysis Division, where her knowledge of Japanese was useful in analyzing Japanese propaganda. Thus in a few years, and during the war, she made the neat jump from internee to employee of a secret agency, which proves to me that something was screwy somewhere.

Later she did graduate work in sociology at the University of Chicago, specializing in race relations, in which she had done a great deal of work, for some years as an employee of the American Council on Race Relations. She speaks, reads and writes Japanese, which was no help to her at all in the job she held when she got married, assistant editor of the official publication of the American Library Association.

She is five feet tall, has brown eyes, black hair, weighs 104 pounds, and has a heavenly disposition. She has more friends—in all walks of life, all races and all creeds—than anyone else I know. She is an extrovert, comic, a Dodger fan, an expert pingpong player, a fair tennis player, and is mad about horses. She expects to be [in] Bucks County sometime next spring.

Having been born in the United States, Mari has always had American citizenship. She has, however, never been in Japan, but we may come home that way after her visit to India. She has been to Bucks County while working at her library job and found the area around New Hope delightful, but very expensive.

Merry Xmas,

Jim

Not long after Jim and Mari arrived back in this country, landing in San Francisco, Jim called me.

"Mari and I are going to buy a car and drive across country, winding up in Chicago. Why don't you and Annie come to Chicago and spend a couple of days, get to know Mari, and then drive home with us?" We were anxious to meet this Mari Sabusawa. So even though it was June, the height of my busiest season, Ann and I flew to Chicago and spent two days there meeting Mari and her brother, Harry Sabusawa.

On the drive back from Chicago, Mari cleared up the mystery that had been bothering me since learning of their wedding. I asked her why Jim hadn't told Ann and me that he was getting married. It seemed peculiar, even for Jim.

"Well, at that time, he didn't know my answer," Mari said. "I told him when he asked that he would have to wait and I would give him an answer later."

I had to give Mari credit for not immediately agreeing to marry Jim. She was beautiful, thirteen years younger than Jim, never married, and Japanese. Jim was a twice-divorced, forty-eight-year-old white Quaker. The issue of "mixed" marriages was very heated in the mid-1950s, and Jim had advised others against getting into what he felt could be very difficult relationships. Later, he and Mari *were* subjected to discrimination, especially when they lived in Hawaii. But Jim was probably the most unprejudiced person I ever met; he was ready to fight discrimination wherever he found it. It was a topic he wrote about until the end of his life, and it was a major theme in *This Noble Land: My Vision for America*, published the year before he died.

That drive back from Chicago was the first of many car trips the four of us would take over the next three decades. Whenever they were at home in Bucks County, Jim and Mari and Ann and I would spend every Tuesday together. Jim would get up very early and work until noon. Then the four of us would meet for lunch, often at my house, before taking off for a drive. We'd head for the Poconos Mountains in northeastern Pennsylvania, or down to the New Jersey shore.

At least once a year, we would make a trip to Atlantic City. This was long before the casinos were built; we would drive down in the fall or spring, when the crowds were light, for a casual stroll on the boardwalk and a whiff of the salty ocean air. Jim would usually go off alone to spend an hour in a store that sold stamps. Once we drove clear to Cape May, on the southern tip of New Jersey, and then back up the Atlantic Coast to Asbury Park in the central part of the state, just to get a look at all the little hamlets and cities that dot the Jersey coast. Later, when Jim and Mari made their home in Maryland or Florida or Maine, we continued the tradition, albeit more sporadically.

During these rides, the friendship between the four of us was cemented. I drove. Jim always sat up front with me, while Ann and Mari sat together in the back seat, enabling the occasional gender-specific topic of conversation. We always joked that you could identify people by class if you could see the way two couples sat together in a car: In the working class, one couple sat in the front seat, and the other couple in the back. In the middle class, the two men sat in the front, and the wives in the back. In the upper classes, one husband sat up front with the other's wife. We were solidly middle-class.

We roamed far and wide, stopping at local landmarks, sometimes to accommodate Jim's research on his latest book. Occasionally, the highlight of a trip would be some hilarious incident or just an unexpected encounter along the road.

On one Tuesday drive through the Reading and Scranton areas of Pennsylvania, we wound up at dusk in Reading. We had heard of a restaurant in Reading called Joe's, famous for the morels and other wild mushrooms that the owner harvested from the local woods, so we asked a man walking his dog to direct us to Joe's restaurant.

He looked at us rather quizzically. "Are you sure you want to go there? It's in a rather rough neighborhood." He suggested other, less well-known restaurants where, he said, the food was better.

But we weren't going to be dissuaded. "Well, if you insist," said the man. "It's down this street two blocks and then left two blocks."

It was a bit of a rough neighborhood, but we found Joe's and walked into an upscale restaurant—Italian, with everything in very good taste. There were starched white napkins on the starched white tablecloths, and expensive table settings and glassware. I ordered a martini and Mari ordered Champagne; neither Jim nor Ann drank.

The waiter arrived with the menu. One glance at the out-of-sight prices told us that we were in the wrong place for a casual dinner as far as Jim and Mari were concerned. We ended up ordering just soup, a "consommé with mushrooms" that turned out to be clear broth with one floating slice of mushroom. From then on, whenever we found ourselves in an expensive restaurant—which didn't happen often when Jim and Mari were along—one of us would remark, "Well, this must be Joe's."

While Jim was writing Caribbean, he and Mari had an apartment in Coral Gables near the Florida Everglades. Ann and I had started spending winters at our condo in Palm Beach, so the four of us were able to resume our sightseeing drives down there. We all continued to spend time in Florida each winter throughout the 1980s, and often the four of us headed into the Everglades to admire the wildlife and natural landscape. Mari was always ready with her camera, insisting at even the most mundane locales, "Oh, let's stop here and take a picture."

Mari must have taken a million pictures. She always had the cheapest camera you could buy, bright orange or purple or blue, which cost about eight dollars at the drugstore. She bought them three and four at a time because "they take the best pictures you ever saw." As a matter of fact, we never saw any pictures Mari took. As far as I know, she never had the film developed.

On one of our trips through the Everglades in April, 1988, Mari took out her camera at a roadside rest station and suggested we have our picture taken on a picnic bench in front of a pond.

"If we're going to take a picture, all four of us should be in it," I said. I noticed a man and woman who had just pulled up in a camper, and asked the man if he would take the photo. We posed while he obligingly focused and snapped the shutter. I thanked him and, of course, identified Jim.

"You mean the guy who wrote *South Pacific*?"

"Yep," I replied.

The man walked to within two feet of Jim and said, "I read that book, *Tales of the South Pacific*. It's because of you I joined the Navy."

When he said that, I panicked for a second. What if he hated the Navy and was going to beat up on Jim? But Jim stood his ground. "How was it?" he asked.

"It was the best thing I ever did," the man said, shaking

Jim's hand. "I stayed in the Navy for twenty-four years, and now I'm retired with a pension that makes it possible for us to drive around and see the world. Thank you."

Naturally, Jim was pleased as punch.

Jim was curious about everything. On that same trip through the Everglades, he noticed a group of people sitting on beach chairs alongside one of the canals. Nearby, there were about a half-dozen cars and pick-up trucks that had been converted into campers.

"Let's go talk to those guys," Jim said. We pulled up, and Jim bombarded the group with questions.

"Where you from?"

"From Michigan, up near the lakes."

"What are you doing here?"

"Oh, we come down here for the winter and live along these canals. In summer we go up and live along the lakes in northern Michigan."

"You mean to say you live in all these places and don't pay rent?" Jim asked.

"Oh no, we never pay rent anywhere. We just migrate to one place and another."

Just like gypsies used to do, I supposed. But they weren't gypsies. They were retirees, one a veteran with a bad leg from shrapnel wounds, another a retired policeman. A couple of them were living on Social Security payments.

"Well," Jim asked, "What do you do for food?"

"Oh, we drive into the local village and buy bread, hot dogs, sliced bologna and stuff. We manage pretty well."

"What do you do about bathrooms?" Jim asked, unwilling to leave any question unasked.

"Well, there's a little church down there—you'll see it if you drive by on that road—that lets us use the bathrooms to wash up and do what we have to do."

Jim was impressed by how these people managed to get by on very little cash.

"Herman, these guys have learned the art of living," he told me. "They're living the way *we* want to, but we're killing ourselves and still not living that way. No property tax, no rent, no electricity bills. They're the modern gypsies, I guess, but they sure have it made."

We rode around like nomads ourselves on these car trips. Time passed quickly because of our conversations. These conversations went on for six or eight hours, often starting at lunch and continuing through dinner. We talked about whatever came to mind—abortion, young people, and, more often than not, politics. Generally, the discussions swirled among the four of us. Ann and Mari were both very vocal, with liberal viewpoints on just about every topic. Jim was initially rather conservative but became more liberal as he grew older. He liked to get Ann—the daughter of a union organizer—riled by starting out, "Well, Annie, what are the unions doing now for the working man?" And off we'd go, both literally and figuratively.

On one drive, we talked about the Holocaust. Jim told of a meeting in Israel with a Jewish family from Berlin, who had twice escaped the Nazis. The first time, the father announced to his family one night at dinner that they were leaving the city before dawn the next day for France because he'd heard a rumor there was to be a roundup of Jews. His wife protested; she had a bridge date with friends. His son objected, saying he had an important tennis lesson later in the week. And his daughter protested, having just accepted a date with a popular boy. But the father was adamant, and the family left Germany for Paris.

Several years later, after the German invasion of France, the father again learned of an imminent roundup of Jews, this time in Paris. He announced at dinner that the family would be leaving at dawn for England. Incredibly, his family again complained about the inconvenience! But once again, the father prevailed, and they left the next morning. The family sat out the war in England, then relocated to Israel. Too few Jews in Berlin and Paris were as far-seeing and fortunate as that man.

On one of our last drives, Jim and I had an impassioned discussion about the love affair between director Woody Allen and Soon-Yi Previn, the eighteen-year-old adopted daughter of actress Mia Farrow, who also had been Allen's lover. Jim's theory was that we can't hold artists like Woody Allen to conventional standards of behavior because it would stifle their creativity. Tennessee Williams couldn't have written plays like *A Streetcar Named Desire* or *Cat on a Hot Tin Roof* if he had lived "normally," said Jim. He mentioned authors Norman Mailer and Truman Capote as other examples.

"You can't expect these people to write the extraordinary things they do if they live ordinary lives," he argued. Of course, Jim insisted that his *own* life be *completely* normal.

Sometimes our conversations became very emotional. During one drive through Bucks County in the autumn of 1973, the issue was censorship.

The Commonwealth of Pennsylvania was trying to respond to public outrage over pornography, which a great many citizens felt was too easily available to youngsters in book and magazine stores. There was also concern by some citizens about the content of some books taught in public schools, including *The Catcher in the Rye* and *The Adventures of Huckleberry Finn*. The state Supreme Court had just ruled that local communities could determine for themselves what constituted pornography. The legislature, reacting to the prospect of every village and township setting its own standards, was trying to pass a statewide anti-pornography law that would be upheld in court. Jim had been asked to testify at hearings in Harrisburg, the state capital; he told us he planned to support the idea of the state regulating the sale of pornographic material.

Ann is much more liberal than I am, and she became very excited and lit into Jim. As a writer, she argued, he was the *one* guy in the world who should never consider *any* kind of censorship; next thing he knew, somebody would be censoring *his* books. She told Jim it would be a disgrace for him to testify in favor of any kind of censorship.

Their argument lasted almost an hour and became very heated. Mari joined in, but I—driving and listening—didn't say much. When we arrived at their house on the hill late in the afternoon, Jim was so disturbed by Ann's attack on him that he got out of the car without saying good-bye.

As it turned out, Ann's arguments had an impact on Jim. He dropped his plan to testify in favor of the censorship bill, and a short time after our day trip, he wrote to us on October 18, 1973, enclosing a newspaper clipping:

Dear Herman and Ann,

The discussion on the way home was most profitable and helped me to clear up my thinking.

The attached news story from Philadelphia summarizes the whole thing. (1) It supports Ann's claim that once the censors feel themselves with a free hand, they'll run wild. (2) It supports my claim that if you leave this at the local level this state will become a madhouse.

You will be pleased to know that in Harrisburg on Thursday, <u>every</u> witness answered when asked by the Chairman, "Are you proposing that an adult shall not be allowed to read whatever he wants in his own home?" that he or she believed the individual could do what he wished without interruption from the state. Some had argued just the opposite in their opening statements, but when asked cold turkey all came down in favor of individual freedom within the home. The argument then centered upon what was being done in public.

Four-fifths of the testifiers supported state-wide operations with the others favoring county-wide.

It was by no means a witch hunt, but the iron-clad woman who had sponsored the bill and who was mainly responsible for rushing it through, never gave an inch. She looked as if she wanted to kill me.

Let's travel again.

Jim

During all the time the four of us spent together, Jim kept

his feelings for Mari private. I never saw him express affection for her in what I thought were the usual ways; I never saw him hug her, or pinch her affectionately in the way that I'd seen among most other couples. They *did* call each other "Cookie." But they weren't physically demonstrative; it wasn't Jim's nature to be affectionate in public.

Jim and Mari could be apart for weeks at a time while he traveled. She was very independent, too; sometimes it was Mari who went away alone on a long trip.

One of Mari's self-appointed tasks, and one of the reasons their marriage worked so well, was to see that Jim was properly taken care of, that his travel tickets were in order and everything was done to make his life easy. She was very protective of him. Jim would say yes to almost anything, whether it was a speaking engagement or a book signing or an appearance at a public event. Usually, it was Mari who would say, "Now wait a minute, Cookie, you can't do that. You've got to be here, you've got to be there." Or, "Cookie, you can't do all of those things." All Jim had to worry about was focusing on his writing.

Sometimes Mari *would* say yes to a request for Jim's time, and join in the fun. After the musical *South Pacific* was released for summer stock productions around the country, local showman St. John "Sinjin" Terrell quickly lined up a summer stock production. Sinjin's musicals were held in a circus tent called The Music Circus in nearby Lambertville, New Jersey.

Sinjin had a great eye for publicity, and he knew just how to boost the box office receipts for his production of *South Pacific*. He asked Jim to play the role of one of the sailors in the scene featuring the song "Bloody Mary Is the Girl I Love," and he persuaded Mari to play a servant to the French planter Emile de Becque.

Jim and Mari agreed to a week's run in the roles. Sinjin made the most of it with his billboards: "See Jim Michener, who wrote *South Pacific, playing* in *South Pacific.*"

Seeing them on stage was hilarious, and the production drew big crowds. When I mentioned it to Oscar Hammerstein II, he said, "Boy, I'd give *anything* to be in one of my plays."

If someone took advantage of Jim, it was Mari who got mad. After he wrote *Sports in America* in 1976, an acquaintance of theirs wrote a book that was very, very similar and made it appear that it had been written by Jim. Though Jim seemed to put it out of his mind, Mari was furious.

Mari knew how to get things done. Once, they were invited on a voyage to the Antarctic, on board a small boat designed to get in close to wherever they wanted to go. Jim and Mari were living in Florida at the time; to make the trip, they had to catch a plane in New York to Rio de Janeiro, then fly to a port further down the South American coast, where at last they could board their ship.

They had been told to bring very warm clothing, hats, and high wading boots, but at the time, they only had light summer clothing on hand. Mari wasn't about to take the time or make the effort to return to Bucks County and search through the house looking for appropriate winter wear. She called a big shot at L. L. Bean, ordered a pile of clothes and equipment, and had the company ship the things directly to their port in South America. Luckily, the clothes arrived the day before they embarked.

Jim and Mari would leave on a half-hour's notice to travel anywhere in the world. They would drop everything and go, and buy whatever clothes they needed along the way. Jim never seemed to have the right clothing to go anywhere; he had so many clothes, but they were never in the right place. Later, when he and Mari donated the house on the hill to Delaware Valley College, six tuxedos were found in the closet. Mari was the same way. She stayed with us once for four or five days and left a suitcase with us—forgot all about it, and never once asked for it.

Jim rarely bought himself anything, except when he went to a discount clothing store in Philadelphia. Mari would say to me, "I like your pants, send me some of those pants for Jim." And after Mari was diagnosed with breast cancer in the mid-70s and underwent a mastectomy, she insisted that Ann buy bras for her. Ann finally persuaded her that it was important for her to have them fitted for herself.

Throughout their travels, while Jim was doing research for his books all over the world, Jim and Mari learned about and lived in all sorts of different cultures for years at a time. But the two of them had strange blank spots when it came to what most other people would consider a normal lifestyle.

In Florida, we'd stop for lunch at cheap cafeterias where you could get a whole lunch for two dollars. Ann and I love wonderful food, but Jim just didn't share that appreciation. In college, he told me, he would go to Horn and Hardart and buy baked beans; he could have eaten just that for the rest of his life.

I don't think Mari ever cooked a meal in her life. She went to Denny's or McDonald's or Burger King or some other fast-food restaurant for her meals. When we visited Mari and Jim at their apartment in Coral Gables or at the house in St. Michaels, there were cases—literally cases—of canned fruit sitting on the kitchen floor. What else they ate, I don't know.

People often complained to me that the Micheners never answered their mail; when Ann and I visited them in Florida, I understood why. Mari's office was piled sky-high with un-opened mail. She said she just didn't have time to answer it all.

Sometimes Mari could be irritating. She expected some-body to take care of her, to do everything for her. When we were in Florida, she would call me from the airport: "Herm, I'm here, come and get me and take me over to Coral Gables." I didn't mind doing this for her, but it bothered me that she expected it.

Jim was always somewhat aloof, even from his best friends. In 1965, he suffered his first heart attack. At the time, the procedures and technology that exist today to enable a quick recovery weren't available, and Jim spent several weeks in Doylestown Hospital, while Mari lived at our house, a few miles away. Throughout Jim's long stay in the hospital, Ann—who had three teenagers and a toddler at home—cooked dinner for him every night and took it over to the hospital. (She later did the same thing for Mari, when Mari had an appendectomy.)

As a gesture of gratitude to all the people who had sent cards and flowers and best wishes for his recovery, Jim had this card printed:

> When a man has his interior world shuttered as
> mine was, it is important for him to know that the

outside world remains as before. Your message from wherever you were helped convey that fact into the hospital and I appreciate it.

Oddly, he didn't send one of those cards to Ann and me. When I mentioned it, he took one of the cards and wrote:

Dear Herman and Ann, I was afraid this was too impersonal for old time friends. If I was wrong, you deserve the first one. Shalom and Aloha.

Jim's way of dealing with a crisis was to study it; during his recuperation from his heart attack, he became an expert on the heart and treatment of heart disease. Even years later, he was keeping up with new developments. Here's an excerpt from a 1967 review he wrote for his publisher, Random House, of a new book on the topic of heart disease. He not only sent me a copy of his analysis; he arranged for Random House to send me a copy of the book.

To be specific, if you have an active young man in his mid-forties on your staff, who is forty pounds overweight, hypertensive with high blood pressure, diabetes, gout, whose father and older brother died of a heart attack, the probability of his having one is so great that he ought to seek out medical advice right away—and I mean this week. There are less dramatic cases representing hundreds of us who . . . fall within the danger zone in one or two specifics. I suspect the most significant thing about Dr. Gertler's book is that

> he is right in believing that if a man in his late forties
> fell within this group there are many steps he could
> take to move himself out of it and thus prolong
> his life.

As long as I knew him, Jim had very few really good friends other than Ann and me and Bill and Betty Nash. When Jim was writing *Kent State,* he met Bill Nash, a banker in the next town over from Kent, Ohio. The Nashes were devoted to doing things for Jim and Mari. They took boat trips together, and Jim had a lot of confidence in Bill as a businessperson. Bill became Mari's financial advisor, and after she died, Bill helped Jim clear up his affairs and sell some of his properties.

Though everyone Jim met wanted to be his friend, Jim didn't really know how to be friends in the usual way, and he never took the trouble to learn. It still irritates Ann that Jim and Mari came to only one of our girls' three weddings. He and Mari never sent a wedding gift to Leda and her husband, and they never responded to our invitations to Jeffra's and Binny's weddings.

I really don't think Jim knew it was important to us that he come. And I wasn't going to tell him.

For myself, I might moan about having to go to the wedding of my grandniece twice-removed, but when it comes down to it, I go. At one wedding, I was complaining to my niece: "What am I doing here? I'm bored stiff, and I don't even know these people getting married." And she said to me, "You have to be here; you're a barracuda in our family." I said, "What? Barracuda? What's that?"

And she said, "You're important in our family."

Ann still hasn't quite forgiven Jim for missing our daughters' weddings, but she told me recently that she believes Jim and Mari were just completely unaware of the nature of family obligations.

"They lived in their own world," she told me. "They never felt responsible to anybody but themselves. I think it came from never having had any family, any roots. There was a complete lack of obligation to anybody else."

Even so, the four of us had very, very good times together.

7. Work

Jim rarely talked about his work, but he never really stopped working; even during our spontaneous, rambling drives through the countryside, he was always stopping to talk to people along the way, asking questions, and doing research for a book he was writing or a book he was thinking about writing.

Jim was very inquisitive, and he had a marvelous memory. He learned almost everything there is to know about landscaping and plants and trees and birds. He knew all about the stars. He knew all about the oceans and the waves. When you had a talk with him, you began to learn that there was very little that Jim didn't know about. He came into contact with many exciting people, but he liked to talk with people in all walks of life. Everyone wanted to meet him, and he wanted to meet everyone.

In the spring of 1989, Jim and Mari were staying at the Sheraton Hotel in Reading, Pennsylvania, while Jim was writing *The Novel*, which was set in the nearby Pennsylvania Dutch country. One day he called and said, "Why don't you and Ann come up here and we'll spend the day together and take a drive?"

Ann and I got there in time for lunch at the hotel. Jim

thought it would be interesting to drive to Pottsville to try to find the house where novelist John O'Hara had lived and see what the real-life setting for "Gibbsville" was like. John O'Hara, the author of *Appointment in Samarra* and one of the most popular writers of the '50s and '60s, had based his novels in Pennsylvania's coal country and Philadelphia's wealthy Main Line suburbs. *From the Terrace* had been made into a feature film starring Paul Newman, and the film version of *10 North Frederick* had starred Gary Cooper.

Sure enough, we found O'Hara's former house in Pottsville and then drove around the area. Jim was interested in knowing what that part of the country looked like. At one time it had been coal mining country, but most of the residents had retired from the mines, and the area had become run down. Most of the young people had left.

We came to a little subdivision where some new homes were being built, and it seemed out of place. Jim wanted to know, since all the young people had left the area, who was going to live there? We drove into the subdivision and met the builder. Jim's curiosity took over: How much does this house cost? How big is it? Who is buying it?

The builder took us all through the subdivision. He had never heard of Jim Michener or of John O'Hara, who had lived only ten miles from where we stood. Jim understood that that's the way it is: Not everyone reads books.

To those who did read his books, Jim was always gracious. Once, many years earlier, I got a call from a friend of mine who had been an optometrist in Philadelphia but who had moved his practice to Ventnor, just outside Atlantic City. The son of a friend of his had just graduated from Swarthmore

College, Jim's alma mater; he was opening a bookstore in Atlantic City, and was hoping I could get Jim to come down to the store for a book signing to give the business a boost.

When I suggested the trip to Jim, he agreed. He was usually willing to help another Swarthmore graduate, and he was always happy to sign his books. Jim also thought that a bookstore could help revitalize Atlantic City's business district, which was deteriorating.

We got to Atlantic City around noon, had lunch with my friends, Dave and Margaret Brezel, then headed for the bookstore. What a fabulous sight greeted us! A line four deep streamed out of the building, down the street, and around the corner. The mayor was there to give Jim the key to the city.

As often happened when Jim showed up to sign books, he was met by people who had gathered up every Michener book they had at home and brought them for him to inscribe. That day Jim sat down about 1:30 and began signing his name. He was still at it five hours later. I guess some people bought books—I hope they did!

Jim was very generous about signing his books, even on cruises; when passengers learned that Jim was going to be aboard, they toted along all the Michener books they owned for him to autograph.

Once, around 1993, Jim and Mari and I were eating at a restaurant in Austin when our waiter approached.

"I have your book here," he said, holding a battered copy of *Iberia*, a nonfiction book Jim had written twenty-five years earlier. The book was so worn that it was coming apart.

"Because of this book, I've been to Spain three times and I always read it again before I go," he said. "I enjoy Spain much more because of your book and was hoping you'd sign it." Naturally, Jim obliged.

Not all book signings were so easy. Every time Jim published a new book, it was featured at Kenny's Newsstand on West State Street in Doylestown. Joe Kenny, who was known as "Mr. Doylestown" until his death at the age of eighty in 1988, was a friend of Jim's, and Jim had been showing up at Joe's bookstore to autograph his books since 1959, when *Hawaii* was published.

When *Chesapeake* came off the presses in 1978, we loaded up the trunk and back seat of Joe's big black Buick with 300 copies and drove with Joe's daughter, Barbara, to Jim's home in St. Michaels so that Jim could sign the books. Joe, Barbara, and I organized an assembly line: Barbara would unpack a book, Joe would open it to the flyleaf, and then Jim would sign and hand it to me to repack. When each box was filled, I carried it out to the car. Jim worked quickly, signing about four books a minute, and afterward we all went to lunch at Joe's expense. Joe got a speeding ticket on the way to the restaurant, but he said it was worth it—he planned on putting a sign in the bookstore window: "Just off the press! Jim Michener's latest book, personally signed." He said all 300 copies would be sold within two weeks.

Not long afterward, on one of our visits to St. Michaels, Jim and Mari took Ann and me to dinner. While we were savoring our crab cakes, one of the other diners recognized Jim, left the restaurant, drove ten miles to a bookstore in Easton, bought a copy of *Chesapeake*, and returned in time to ask Jim for his autograph.

Jim once joked that he had signed so many of his books

that, in the future, the ones that he *hadn't* signed would be the most valuable.

Sometimes there were complaints about the length of his books. The manuscript for *Alaska*, which was published in 1988, was so thick that his publisher, Random House, suggested that he hold out a certain chapter and add other material to it to create a companion book. That book became *Journey*, a fascinating tale told in about 200 pages about a group of Englishmen who cross Canada heading for the Klondike, where gold had been discovered in the foothills of the mountains near Calgary. Even so, the finished version of *Alaska* ran more than 1,000 pages.

Another of Jim's smaller books is a book of less than 200 pages called *My Lost Mexico*. It was published in 1992, right after *Mexico*, and it explains why he put *Mexico* on hold for twenty-five years.

One night around 1990, I got a call from Jim: "Herman, I'm going to have Virginia go up on the hill and look through our stuff in the gallery."

The house in Pipersville was closed, but Virginia Trumbell, Jim's cousin, had lived there earlier to maintain it while Jim and Mari were away. The gallery Jim had added to the house to hold paintings was also used as a storage room.

"I'm going to ask Virginia to go up there and see if she can find the manuscript on Mexico that I wrote and put aside," Jim said. "I've contacted the Library of Congress, where a lot of my stuff is stored, and they can't find it. I don't know what happened to it. It's an unfinished manuscript, and I want to finish it now. I've got some good ideas."

He added, "If she could stay at your house, I'd appreciate

it."I responded that certainly Virginia could stay with us; Ann and I were very fond of her. The next day around noon, Virginia arrived and asked for the key to the house.

"Come back here and stay with us and have dinner if you like," I suggested.

"Herman," she said, "I'm not coming down from that hill until I find that manuscript."

The gallery was stacked with boxes of artifacts and memorabilia that Jim and Mari had shipped home from their travels to Japan, China, Indonesia, Sri Lanka, Guatemala, and other locations around the world. Whenever they found something they wanted to keep, they'd ship it to Pipersville and it would end up in the gallery, perhaps never to be opened.

It apparently took some doing, but eventually, in a carton buried under a lot of other boxes, Virginia found what she was looking for. The carton wasn't even marked "Mexico," but something else. Virginia said, "I just looked into every box I could find."

Jim was very grateful for her efforts, and as a result, *Mexico* was completed and published, as was *My Lost Mexico*. If you're curious about what made Jim stop writing *Mexico* twenty-five years earlier, and about the chapters that don't appear in that book, I recommend that you read *My Lost Mexico*.

Of course, short books such as *Journey* and *My Lost Mexico* were exceptions for Jim, and even I complained to him once about the length of most of his books. But he wasn't offended, and he gave me some practical advice:

"Herman," he said, "just skip the first hundred pages. I only write them for the historians."

8. At Home in the World

Jim and Mari traveled extensively, and even when they weren't traveling, they often lived for years at a time at whatever location Jim was researching for his latest book.

We kept in touch by letter, but Jim couldn't get my address right. Early on, before zip codes, he'd send mail to "Herman Silverman, Pool Builder, Doylestown, Pennsylvania." Or he'd write to me at Rural Delivery 4, or Durham Hill, or Danboro Pike, or Cross Keys—none of them having anything to do with my actual address. Somehow, I always received his mail, but his letter invariably arrived with a sticker advising me to notify the sender of my proper address.

Jim's letters, pounded out single-spaced on one of the typewriters he always had at hand wherever he lived, are as vivid as when he first wrote them. This excerpt is from a five-page missive written in 1955, after rioters had stormed the Majestic Hotel in Saigon where Jim was staying:

> It was (and is) pretty horrible. At least I found out whether or not I had guts. I stayed here in the Majestic and listened to them coming down my hall. They completely annihilated the room next door and then started in on mine. I thought the lock would hold, but

it didn't, so when the door crashed in I stood with my typewriter and said, "I'm an American writer. Behave or I'll write bad things about you." They stood there for a second and then we all laughed.

As I write this, quite shaken up, a little boy stands guard at my door. . . . Whether anyone has been killed I can't say, but this has really been a jolt. All the rooms around me have gone now, and I've been standing in the doorway smiling limply and saying in as firm a voice as my quaking knees and throbbing heart would permit, "American." Today it's been a damned good word. . . .

Brother Herman, if I sound casual about this, I ain't. Only my determination not to let the gang in after the door went down saved things here and if one of those wild men with the clubs had said "Boo" I'd have fainted.

Because Jim's letters are so interesting, I've included a selection of them here, with little comment. Like so much of Jim's writing, his letters—like this one to me and to two other friends—speak for themselves.

Kabul, Afghanistan
June 5, 1955

Dear Hobart Lewis, Leonard Lyons,
Herman Silverman,

I'm smuggling this letter out of a wild and wonderful nation, so the political comment contained herein is completely confidential.

We have been very close to war here several times
in the past few weeks and it is still quite possible that
it may break out sometime this summer. The reasons
are almost comic opera, but the results could be cata-
strophic. The country is ruled by one family and the
present power is the cousin of the king. He is neither
pro-West nor pro-Russian, but because his two neighbors are pro-American (Iran and Pakistan) he is
thrown into the pro-Russian camp. He uses this position . . . to try to squeeze the democracies, and he
succeeds. He has pretty well convinced his people that
they can have a <u>little</u> Russian help without being
forced to accept a total domination.

I must say that Russia has behaved pretty admirably
in this sorry mess, for by taking even casual steps, I am
sure the Russians could throw this nation into either
war or revolution, either of which would be an invitation for her to take over. Russia's moderation here is
the only reason I have seen to cause hope that her
moderation in Europe is also sincere; but cynics point
out that here she has no chance of losing, since the
nation must sooner or later fall into her orbit. I think
there's a fighting chance that because of Russia's desire
to show herself a reasonable nation in Europe, she may
act reasonably in Afghanistan also; andthat, in the time
thus saved, the democracies may accomplish the good
programs upon which they are already launched.

War between Afghanistan and Pakistan could disrupt all this. Then the US would probably be drawn in
on Pakistan's side and Russia would surely sweep into

Afghanistan, take it over and thus be within a few miles of a seaport on the Indian Ocean. I really shiver to think how close we have been to this major calamity recently.

The war party of Afghanistan shocks me by admitting to me that (1) they aren't sure what their objectives are; (2) they don't know what peace terms they are fighting for; (3) they don't believe Pakistan would dare to use air power; (4) that Russia could easily lick all the rest of the world; (5) but they don't like Russia and she would have to get out after the fighting was over. To plunge this part of the world into war on such feeble logic would be appalling.

That war was avoided, we feel, was due to the extremely sharp representations made by all foreign ministers in Kabul, probably including the Russian, who did not want any of his European apple carts upset at such a time. A second contributing factor must have been the brilliant behavior of American ministers in Kabul, Delhi and Karachi. A third has been the very cautious behavior of the Pakistanis, who certainly don't want war on their western front while they are engaged with India on the east. A fourth has been the instant intervention by all Muslim powers, who openly state they would deplore a Muslim-Muslim war. But most important to me has been the complete switch of India, which covertly supported the Afghans so long as they were mere nuisances to Pakistan, but who appear to have tried vigorously to stop the war when it seemed likely that Russia might take over both Afghanistan and Pakistan and thus stand astride the gates to India.

In short, we in Kabul have seen a lot of nations acting very quickly and very maturely to stop a major war. That's good. The daily alarms however have been trying. At one point we were all near evacuation. I was present when a secret service agent from one of the embassies reported that the looting of Kabul (by local tribesmen) had been set for a given day. And a malcontent soldier was picked up who told us that his company had earmarked all the best houses to loot them before the tribesmen got there first. It has been a weird and wonderful month.

I am about half-way through my stay here, and wish it could be indefinitely prolonged. This is a magnificent place for a writer. The other day two policeman got into a fight over their mutual love for a young dancing boy and one stabbed the other to death. The government thereupon turned the murderer over to the father of the slain man. This old man tied the murderer to the ground, then with a rusty scimitar cut his throat while about a hundred approving spectators watched in the public square. I'm not supposed to know anything about this, but a photographer who was present asked the old man with the knife to "work from the other side of the throat so the sun will be better." He slipped me a copy of this gentle scene. I almost heaved my cookies. (This highly confidential till I leave.)

But writing is tough these days, what with Rourk and Hemingway preempting Africa, Justice Douglas and Lowell Thomas speaking for Asia, and Nordhoff and Hall in charge of the Pacific. You will be interested to know, however that I am the first writer ever to have climbed the Hindu Kudh in bifocals.

Tomorrow I start on a caravan across the desert aptly named The Desert of Death. (This whole nation is almost a Hollywood script.) And when I get back I'll try to take one trip up to the Russian border and then to work . . . horrible thought.

Warmly,

Jim

The following spring, as Jim and Mari traveled aboard a freighter bound for Honolulu, Jim wrote to my brother and me and our wives about the presidential election campaign:

En route, Hawaii

April 21, 1956

Dear Ira and Mattiemae, Herman and Ann,

No business, but a leisurely report on a long and delightful trip. Mari and I are sweating it out on a real tug with fine companions on a ten-day crossing from Japan to Hawaii. Our ship is small, a freighter carrying lumber from Manila to New York, and the food is good. We spend lots of our time trying to get a sun tan, or sleeping. We manage about 16 hours of the latter each day.

We got the books Ira wanted, but as per the enclosed invoice, they were both hard to get and

somewhat expensive. They are extremely lovely, however, and I can understand why you wanted them. We
got no prints, since the order reached us quite late, but
we can get almost anything you want mailed
promptly upon our return, when we can ascertain just
what you want. That way you won't waste money . . .
and I can get them for you wholesale!

We spent money like crazy and had a magnificent
time, including a fantastic tiger hunt with an Indian
maharajah, trips everywhere, and a lot of hard work. I
would advise you two boys never to take your wives to
Colombo, Delhi, Bangkok, Hongkong, Kyoto, Tokyo or
Honolulu. In fact about as far as I'd go right now is the
Quakertown farmer's market. You'd better get our
New Hope properties on a dividend paying basis
quick, or we may have to move in with you . . . .

Traveling on this ship makes me think [General
Dwight D.] Eisenhower is a shoo-in. We haven't met a
Democrat yet, and the reasons for voting Republican
are the solid ones that make any attack on Ike so difficult. The most persuasive arguments so far have been
these: "Ike never swore in office the way Truman did
with that newspaper fellow." "You don't see Ike's son
trying to get rich while his father is president. He's an
honest soldier, not a TV star like Margaret Truman."
"General Eisenhower has promised us that he would-
n't whistle stop this year. I think the way Truman went
across the country asking people to vote for him was
humiliating to the presidency." "After [Secretary of
State Dean] Acheson balled up the foreign policy it

took [John Foster] Dulles almost four years to straighten it out, and we ought to see that the same team stays in for four more years." "You can trust Ike's cabinet. They're all businessmen." "If he's willing to run again and risk his health for us, the least we can do is send him back with a bigger vote than last time." "Everybody who speaks against Richard Nixon is a communist, because he was the one who got the communists out of government." And most crushing of all: "Adlai Stevenson is an egghead."

I hope you are all having a good time. We land in Honolulu on April 25, in California about June 15, in Doylestown ten days later. Business in Chicago might disrupt this, but we plan to be home by then and stay for quite a long stretch.

Warmly,
Jim

Jim wasn't immune to the dangers inherent in all this travel, as this next exchange of letters makes clear. When I wrote to him, Jim was staying at the Imperial Hotel in Tokyo, but as usual, he didn't stay there long.

October 18, 1957

Dear Jim:

Just a short note to let you know how happy we are that you escaped any injury in the airplane accident. I guess I was the first one to know about what had happened to you—almost as soon as you knew about it.

As you know it first came across the news wire without any details at about 7 o'clock in the A.M. My phone started ringing and all the local Philadelphia newspapers were calling me, trying to get information about you and Mari. Mari was in New York at the time, seeing the World Series—so they couldn't get to her too well.

Ann and I went up to see the sixth game of the Series. Although I am not much of a baseball fan, I must admit it was rather interesting for me and, of course, Ann was very excited about the game.

I'm sorry I didn't get a chance to say goodbye before you left. Of course, I want to wish you all the luck in the world on this assignment.

Annie and I and Mari have been out a couple of times to a few of the local shows, and I must admit you have got yourself a real find in that broad. The weather here has been very warm, and the 30-day forecast calls for warmer then normal and more rain than normal—both of these we can use to great advantage.

Keep well, best regards from Annie and the kids,

Herman

Singapore, Nov. 10, 1957

Dear Herman,

That was a very thoughtful letter you sent me to Japan, and I appreciate it very much. Actually, the accident disturbed me very little, because if you walk away from one like that, you feel so completely relieved that other things don't matter a great deal. I certainly feel good and appear to be in excellent health. But I'm still surprised that you can fly a plane at 96 miles an hour smack into the ocean and not kill everybody. Try it with a tree sometime!

I hope your business continues to do reasonably well. There's so much summer out here that I forget winter is descending upon you. I trust it finds you in a good cash position and that you can sweat out the long cold weeks. It seems like that's always a problem for all of us.

America has been very badly damaged by Sputnik, but more by Little Rock. People over here ask an American about little else, and I'm afraid we'll have more of them in the future. What nonsense!

Please give my best to Ann and the children. I'll see you soon. Mari meets me this week here in Singapore, then we go to work up-country.

Warmly,

Jim

Columnist Leonard Lyons urged the Micheners to visit Israel in 1963 to get acquainted with that emerging country. They did make the trip, and Jim became so fascinated with Israel that he decided to make it the subject of his next book. He and Mari lived there for two years while he did research. When *The Source* was published in 1965, people all over the world read it and began to grasp the problems facing the Middle East.

Jim presented Ann and me with a first edition of *The Source,* and inscribed the flyleaf with this note:

At the Silvermans—Bucks County 12 June 65
To the Silvermans, who have been with me through
the writing of many works—only to have me write a
special one for them at last.

Shalom,

Jim Michener

Ann and I were so inspired by Jim's book that we took our
four daughters to Israel the next summer. With our letters of
introduction from Jim we were treated like royalty. In Haifa,
we were given an entire floor of the Dan Carmel Hotel, and
when the manager learned that we were celebrating the thir-
teenth birthday of our daughter, Binny, she even arranged
for a birthday cake and presented Binny with an antique sil-
ver charm.

Except for a brief television travel assignment, Jim never
returned to Israel and never talked much about it.

"I never go back," he once told another writer.

No matter how far he was from home, Jim kept up to date on
news from home, particularly political news. He sent this letter from Haifa to Ann and me and a Pipersville friend:

May 11, 1963

Dear Mary and Herman and Annie,

Since you both have children, we thought you'd
appreciate this story . . . .

We had a good time in London (cold) and a better
in Naples (expensive). We took the Amalfi drive which

is certainly one of the most beautiful in the world. The guide says in a hushed voice, "That village up there is where Mrs. [John F.] Kennedy lived last summer." Now it's the most popular spot on the trip.

The Rocky [Nelson A. Rockefeller] [re]marriage jolted us all. The guy has guts but he may also have killed his chances for the [presidential] nomination. Local papers play up real big the threat of the church to discipline the minister who did the dirty deed.

Well, we got aboard the Jewish ship S.S. Jerusalem (marvelous) where we had a great time (didn't even notice it was all kosher, which means no butter, nothing hot on Sunday, but Mari quite killed everyone by asking, 'Did you cook the chicken in milk, it's so tender?').

There was one other couple that seemed gentile, a handsome businessman from California and his rather standard middle class (upper brackets) wife, and they certainly didn't appear to be having a very good time. In fact, he was gloomy. So Mari went over to him to pass the time of day and he said, "We're going to Israel for a special reason. We land on Friday, and we're heading right for a kibbutz. Last year our daughter said, when she graduated from college, 'Dad, I'd like to work for a year in a kibbutz.' I hadn't ever heard the word and I wasn't even aware that the Jews had a country. But anyway, she went to Israel, much against our wishes."

When he told me the story (because I thought Mari had it all wrong) he looked out to sea, then added, "Last month she wrote and told us that she had fallen in love with a bright young Jew who worked in the kibbutz, and they were going to get married. We tried by cable to stop it, but could do nothing. So, when we land on Friday we head for the kibbutz, meet the young man on Saturday, and give our daughter away on Sunday. Some Mother's Day!"

I considered the problem for some time and asked what the young man intended doing when he got to the States. "They're not coming," he replied. "They've decided to live in Israel." The poor guy looked as if a ton of cement, wet, had landed on him, so Mari did her best to cheer him up, as did I, and we had some long talks about the future but I must admit that he and his wife were facing problems that were fairly tough on a average minded California couple.

When we left them on the dock they seemed excited and somewhat reconciled to the wild change that had come into their lives. I consoled him by pointing out that the greatest man who ever lived except Jesus, married a Negro woman. He was stunned so I said, "Read it for yourself. Numbers xii, verses 1 etc." And if he read his Bible he would find that what I told him was true.

Of all the people coming to the new land, he and his wife were to us the most appealing, because no other story so heightened the story of what goes on here. The kibbutz ideal has a very powerful effect upon young people, but fortunately most of them contract marriages somewhat less bizarre than this.

We're settled down in very comfortable quarters

and hope that both the Places and the Silvermans will come to visit us in the course of the next year. So far we've discovered a great place to get blintzes, but no place for tennis.

Love to all,

Mari and Jim

Mari added this postscript:

P.S. Mediterranean trip from Naples to Haifa was too short—Only 2 days. Treated royally on board—Sat at Captain's table. Word had gotten around here that Mitch was returning. I am described in local press as "his Hawaiian wife." A number of American writers here at hotel. Our address will be the DAN CARMEL HOTEL, HAIFA, ISRAEL, for time being. Mitch has already gone to work and we get to Tiberias tomorrow. Weather at moment similar to Hawaii's. Today is Shabbat and I will have to orient my week accordingly. Going back to Naples for a minute. Traffic is so bad that we had to find a place to eat (our hotel served only breakfast) without crossing the street. Didn't think we would make it to Haifa! Write us—Mail is most welcome.

Love, Mari

"his Hawaiian wife"

Jim and Mari had been living in Israel nearly six months when Jim wrote to me about the American presidential and gubernatorial election campaigns.

Dan Carmel, Haifa, Israel
October 28, 1963

Dear Herman,

. . . You were the first to say what I've been fearing about the forthcoming election. If [Arizona Senator Barry] Goldwater runs, the wormy ones will really come creeping out of the woodwork, hoping that he might make it. It will be a hideous election, not because he would want it that way, but because of the festering sores that would be laid open. The events, which local newspapers featured, of Adlai being clobbered and spat upon in Texas are a small foretaste.

Whether Goldwater could win or not I don't know. I suspect that if he did win he would make a fairly decent president and most of the crap he's talking now would be forgotten, either by his wishes or because of the pressures of our system. But the electioneering itself would be pretty gruesome, and I for one could not stand aside and see [President John F.] Kennedy defeated by such people. I'll be home.

I hope Milt [Milton J. Shapp] wins [the Pennsylvania gubernatorial election], although Walter Farley—if the Demos pick up only one seat—would be a strong man too. I suspect anti-Jewish feeling will hurt Milt somewhat, but most of that breed is Republican anyway, so I suppose it won't hurt much. He's a fine aggressive, honest fellow and I do wish him a world of luck. . . .

Yes, you and Annie are invited here for a stay at a great hotel. You can also re-charge your religious batteries and go home wearing a yarmulke. The other day a woman and a little child were waiting to cross the street in Haifa. The little kid asks in perfect Hebrew, "is it time to cross now, mother?" She replies in Yiddish, "Wait for the green light." A friend asks, "If you speak Hebrew and your little boy speaks Hebrew, why do you answer him in Yiddish?" The mother replies "I want him to grow up knowing that he's Jewish."

Come along, and bring St. John [Terrell] with you.

Most warmly,

Jim

Mari added:

The ultra Orthodox Jews have been stoning cars again on the Sabbath (This is the group which doesn't recognize Israel as a state & do not speak Hebrew—which they say is a sacred language—they speak Yiddish.) Now last week they vandalized the Ministry of Education building & did all the things—broken windows, damaging desks & furniture, etc. The gov't says they have been doing all they can, but the policemen have been stoned. No one killed so far, just injuries, etc.

The non-religious ones who do not approve of this (the violence) & the Orthodox ones who do not approve of the stoning still seem not to want to raise the issue too strongly—altho the local Jerusalem Post had a good editorial on it this morning. The group causing this trouble are a very small number—they're the boys with the curls & long black coats etc. A revolting bunch of archaic bums! Let me know if I've been censored!!!

Shalom, Mari

The following spring, Jim and Mari left Israel, but as they often did, they took their time getting home, traveling by way of Turkey, Greece, Italy, France, Norway, and even Russia.

August 21, 1964
Oslo, Norway

Did you get our card from Russia? Never sure what gets out. Mitch participated in Am-Sov conference chaired by Norman Cousins. Subject—Disarmament & Cultural exchange, etc.

Love Norway—Mitch suffered spiritual defeat, he says—this is not the land of the famous "smorgasbord" that's Sweden! But they do have huge cold buffet for breakfast and Mitch doesn't eat breakfast.

Sayonara,
Mari and Jim

Even after they returned home, Jim and Mari never stayed in one place for long. Just a sampling of their postcard greetings from their travels over the years is like a world tour.

October 6, 1966
Cordoba, Spain

This is a <u>hotel</u> in Spain. So you can see we're slum-
ming it. We miss you and the kids. Give them our love
. . . . I'm worried sick about the movie Hawaii. I've read
only one review and it was a positive one—by a very
conservative old timer Hawaiian, and if <u>he</u> likes it
we're in trouble so pray for us.
Love, Mich and Mari

Some were written in Mari's handwriting, such as these
two, signed "Mari and Jim":

November 7, 1967
Singapore

Great changes since we were here about 9 years
ago. Great trip—Am only woman officially invited on
trip—66 men and 1 P.R. S.A.S. woman. Win or lose,
we've invited the press for drinks to Raffles Hotel
tonite!!

June 24, 1969
Portugal

"You should have come last week—the sun was
out etc."—We have had all kinds of weather and Mari
has had the flu and we both have had. tummy
troubles. We've been meeting all lines of Portuguese—
Counts, Barons, Dukes, Marquis . . . . We had dinner

with King Umberto of Italy (in exile here)—he was at
the next table . . . .

Long after *Hawaii* was published in 1959, Jim and Mari
continued to return to the islands.

(Undated, from Hawaii; probably 1970 or 1971)
Dear Herm and Annie,
    We've all signed up for hula classes.
Jim Michener and Mari

(Undated, from Hawaii)
Herman and Ann,
    This island was created for you. Relaxation, con-
genial people, perpetual summer, and plenty of
beautiful land at $35,000 per acre!
Love from Vit, Jim and Mari

January 20, 1970
Angkor, Cambodia
    Well, we made it here. Great sight—now our prob-
lem is transportation out. Wish us luck.
Best,
Mari and Jim

December 18, 1975
Okinawa, Japan

On the spur of the moment, the government sent Mari and me out here to represent the U.S. at a splendid World's Fair. It was a unique experience and we loved it.

See you soon,
Jim Mich.

(1977)
Paris, France

Lunch at St. Michael's, flight to Dulles, Concorde to a late dinner in Paris. Superb flight. Small seats. Great food. Travel at its best.

Jim Mich. and Mari

September 21, 1977
Granada, Spain

We filmed here yesterday. Sunny and quite warm. Going smoothly—small towns we knew 7 years ago are now cities. Off to Poland for four days, back to Madrid and France.

Adios
Jaime and Mari

July 16, 1980
Jo'Burg, South Africa

Physically a beautiful country. One T.V. channel and they're watching "Dallas!" Had ostrich scrambled eggs and ostrich steak for lunch.

Love,

Mari and Jim

August 29, 1985
Top of the World Hotel, Alaska

Marvelous Aleutians trip. Jim almost got left behind in Little Drimede in the Aleutians. . . . Would like to see Barrow in winter. Cool and pleasant now.

Love,

Mari and Jim

November 4, 1986
Leicester, England

This is a lovely place to relax and eat delicious food. Countryside is beautiful. Came from Yorkshire country over the hills and valleys.

Love,

Mari and Jim

In 1972, Jim had joined the press horde that accompanied President Richard Nixon on his historic visit to China. When Jim returned to Pennsylvania, Ann and I had lunch with him and Mari at the Candlewick Inn near Red Hill in neighboring Montgomery County so he could tell us about his trip.

After lunch, he gave me a little red book, *Quotations of*

Chairman Mao, which Premier Chou En-lai had handed out as souvenirs to the press. Jim inscribed his copy to me:

1 March 1972

To Herman Silverman
This book was given to James A. Michener
in Peking, China, by Chou En-Lai
on 27 February 1972.

J.A.M.

Wherever he went in the world, Jim had a keen eye for local customs and color. Sometimes he viewed those customs with light-heartedness and compared them with customs from our own youth or those of my teenage daughters; other times, what he learned affected him deeply.

2-13-D Playamar
Torremolinos, Espana
7 March 69

Dear Herman and Ann,

I sent a letter to Leda the other day advising her not to overlook smoking cornsilk, which was the big thing when I was a kid.

Mari and I have been in Marrakech with the hippies, where they sell Marijuana by the kilo! In plastic bags! And in little green almond cookies which knock you right on your kezoo.

When we get home we want to meet your travel

consultant! Rain, rain, rain in Spain. In Morocco, floods the worst they've ever seen, snowstorms, and one hell of an earthquake. The clothing I really need is a damned good parka, and no kidding. If Mari hadn't brought her heavy suede coat she'd have perished by now. But it's all fun. That Marrakech!

Thank you for having sent the news clipping about the election reform. Tell Dave [Appel] my book [*Presidential Lottery, The Reckless Gamble in Our Electoral System*] is coming out at exactly the right time and that the majority of the professional experts are ultimately going to be on my side. It's a pretty well-reasoned statement and not at all radical in its conclusions. I disagree with Nixon "on specifics" but support him in his general approaches.

As of this night we are all worried about what [French President Charles] de Gaulle is going to do about the franc. Rumor here has it that he is totally pissed off at being forced to devalue and will cut the franc not the recommended 10% but a crashing 20%, whereupon everybody else will be in one hell of a stew. We were told today that Spain and England will have to cut too, but we wait.

                              Jim Mich.

Mari added:

We leave Torremolinos the 1st of April & will be in Seville, Spain at the Hotel Alfonso XIII until April 21. Then to Italy for 3 weeks—back to Spain (Madrid), pick up our other 2 bags—on to Lisbon & I shall come home end of May or take the boat on June 2 if they're not booked full. Mitch will go down to Angola and Mozambique for some more research. . . .

We were lucky that earthquake wasn't worse—Lisbon had it bad. I was scared stiff. I prayed first to Allah—it was his territory—then to God & before I got to Buddha, it died down. 3 minutes is a long time!

The next letter, addressed to Mari's brother, to me, and to six other friends, indicates that the earthquake caused Jim and Mari to think about their own mortality.

Hotel Alfonso XIII
Sevilla, España
Easter Sunday, 1969

Dear Friends,

This is Easter in Sevilla, and there has been much talk of death and burial. We therefore thought it appropriate to send each of you a brief statement of our thinking on these matters, in view of the fact that sometime you might be required to know what our wishes were regarding these matters.

If we or either of us should die while we are abroad or away from home, we specifically wish to be buried within a few miles of where-ever we die. Most specifically, we do not wish to have our bodies flown anywhere for any purpose whatsoever.

Next there was an asterisk, and, at the foot of the page, this handwritten note: "Mari would prefer a simple Christian service." The letter continued:

> We may be buried in any kind of cemetery which local custom provides, under the auspices of any church or religion that will tend to the matter, and under any circumstances that might arise. We can be cremated, or buried at sea, or anything else.
>
> We say these things because we have lived in many parts of the world and have found them all congenial. We have been at home with all colors of people, all kinds of nations, all religions and we would be most content to be buried among whatever people or customs we happened to be visiting at the moment. In death we would feel equally at home in all regions of the world, for in life we made all regions our residence and considered ourselves citizens of all parts.
>
> Let us be totally specific about this, lest there be any misunderstanding. We want to be buried where we die, in the simplest manner possible, content with the idea that any area we have ever known or shall know in the future will be home to us.
>
> If the question ever arises and you are in a position to give advice as to what our wishes were, you have this letter to guide you, written on Easter Day.
>
> Most warmly,
>
> James A. Michener
>
> Mari Sabusawa Michener

9. *Politics*

So many of my memories of Jim revolve around politics. We met at a political event, and spent the better part of our time together over the next fifty years debating the political issues of the day. Jim was the only person I ever really enjoyed talking with about politics. We didn't always agree, but we both had a deep interest in the subject, and each of us was always willing to listen. Sometimes, one of us would actually change the other's mind.

Jim's interest in politics increased during his lifetime. His letters from South Africa, Afghanistan, China, and Russia are full of his observations about the politics of those countries. At home, he campaigned for John F. Kennedy in 1960, and in 1962 he even ran for Congress.

Like most people in Bucks County in those days, Jim grew up as a Republican. Ann and I considered him rather conservative when we first met, and he voted for Eisenhower twice. Mari was more liberal than Jim, and gradually, Jim became less conservative. By 1960 he had become a Democrat, and I viewed him as a middle-of-the-road liberal.

In 1996, Jim received a prestigious award from the Bucks County Democrats. He did not attend, but in his letter of acceptance, which I read for him, he remembered Kennedy:

15 June 1996

Mr. Milton Berkes, Chairman
Democratic Party of Bucks County
17 West Court Street
Doylestown, PA 18901

Dear Milt,

I am deeply honored by the invitation from the
Democratic Party of Bucks County to receive the John
F. Kennedy Humanitarian Award. This gives me a
chance to recall my various relationships with that iri-
descent young politician, Jack Kennedy. And although
I was with him in his moments of triumph, I also have
a stab of pain when I think of how close I came to losing the election for him.

An ardent Kennedy supporter enlisted Stan Musial,
Arthur Schlesinger Jr., and the actors Angie Dickinson,
Shelley Winters and Jeff Chandler. We toured the
backwaters of the United States for twenty days, hit-
ting areas where local candidates for the House and
Senate were having trouble getting press attention.

We put on a great show and helped them consid-
erably. We were less fortunate in our attempts to help
Kennedy, the head of the ticket. We operated in some
dozen states, attracting great crowds and much favorable attention. But every state in which we worked
finally voted for Nixon; and someone pointed out
ungraciously that if we had visited two more states
Kennedy would have lost the election.

He forgave me and Musial and nowhere in my biographies prepared by others is it mentioned that Kennedy appointed me national director of the agency which was giving our surplus farm goods to foreign countries to help them feed their people and at the same time put together a strong infrastructure.

I served in this position for some five years but accomplished very little. We found we could not give away surplus farm materials because too many restrictions were imposed both in the United States and in the recipient countries. But we tried and Kennedy thanked me for my efforts.

In appreciation of my work it was rumored that he was going to appoint me Ambassador to Korea. But I pointed out to his staff that since I had a Japanese wife I might not be welcome in Korea and the appointment fell through.

I was with Jack at a dinner party in Washington on the eve of his inauguration. And I saw the beginning of his presidency. That it was cut so short was a terrible tragedy and one from which our nation suffered.

I am honored to be with you tonight and hope that we can revitalize our adherence to the Kennedy tradition.

Sincerely,
Jim Michener

It may have been Kennedy's presidential campaign that prompted Jim to run for Congress. In 1962, Jim had just returned from living in Hawaii and was between books, and, as far as I know, no one else in Bucks County was willing to run against Willard S. Curtin, a Republican lawyer who had represented the 8th congressional district for twelve years. I told Jim I would help in any way I could.

By coincidence, Milton Berkes, a childhood friend of mine who later became chairman of the Democratic Party of Bucks County, arrived on the scene. Milt had been teaching school in Philadelphia, and we became reacquainted after having been out of touch for many years. He knew that Jim and I were friends, and when he heard that Jim was running for Congress, Milt offered to take a leave of absence from the school system to serve as Jim's manager. Jim agreed.

Mari was dead set against Jim's running; she even threatened to go to work for the Republicans if he did run. But once he decided to run, she worked as hard as anybody to get him elected.

I lent Jim a station wagon for his campaign. Even though Jim was shy, he and Milt traveled tirelessly all over the county. Ann arranged coffee meetings for him with local Democratic leaders while I concentrated on fund-raising. I helped plan a dinner in New York with about fifty of Jim's friends, several of whom confided to me that they weren't crazy about the idea of Jim giving up writing for public service; they didn't want to sacrifice their future reading for the good of the country. But they contributed anyway.

Anyone who knows me knows that I am not shy when it comes to raising money for a good cause, and I solicited money for Jim in any way I could. Here's a typical letter dated October 22, 1962, which I sent to Pearl (Buck) Walsh:

As you know, Jim Michener is running for Congress on the Democratic Ticket in the 8th Congressional District of Bucks and Lehigh Counties. You may not know that Jim wants this office very much and is working as if his life depended on it.

Each day he is on the road campaigning for every vote he can get. In Quakertown, a woman called the local paper to report an impostor, who claimed to be James Michener, was at the A & P shaking hands with the shoppers, and she knew that Mr. Michener would never do this. SHE WAS DEAD WRONG. This is exactly what he is doing, shaking hands at Super Markets and speaking at coffee klatches and at various club and organization meetings.

Does he stand a chance? The odds are 5–3 against him on the registration, but to Jim this is an advantage. I know of nothing that stimulates Jim more than an odd-off challenge.

The word is out—Jim Can Win. A local newspaper editor told me that Jim stood an excellent chance, and this editor was a Republican.

All the newspapers in both counties happen to be Republican. In Allentown, the paper is committed to his opponent. How then can Jim get the message to the people? By speaking to as many people as possible, and this he is doing day and night, and through buying space in the papers and printing brochures. This costs money.

Jim needs money for his campaign, and he needs it desperately. Not being a politician, he can't expect funds from persons who usually support politicians.

Then how does Jim raise campaign funds?—from his friends, of course. You know Jim wouldn't ask for help, and yet he is the first person we turn to when we need help and counsel.

I am trying to raise a $5,000 fund from Jim's friends. Some I know, some I don't, but we all know Jim and we have a chance to show him our support in the best way possible.

Please—send Jim a check today. Make it bigger than you can afford. I am contacting 30 of Jim's personal friends and there is not a rich one among them. Make it payable to Michener for Congress Committee. Mail it to: James A. Michener

P.O. Box 125

Pipersville, PA

If Jim wins, you will have the satisfaction of knowing that you sent a good man to Congress. If he loses, you will enjoy the feeling that you supported Jim when he needed it.

Plenty of people wondered why Jim would bother to run in such a Republican-dominated county. And there were those who wondered why he would run at all, considering he was by then a wealthy man living an enviable life. But Jim cared about the issues, and he cared about the country. People who knew him knew that he would take his job as congressman very seriously.

Jim lost the race to Willard Curtin by a fairly large margin. I think he was greatly disappointed, though he never showed it. He had really hoped for the chance to serve in Congress, and he was looking forward to the challenge. In later years, after he got over the disappointment, he liked to claim that he lost the election because of 300 feet of sewer pipe: He joked that a ward leader, a woman in a highly Democratic neighborhood, was supposed to deliver the votes that would have put him over the top, but she made a decision to sit out the election after the Republicans connected her house to the sewer system.

When Jim lost, we were all very sorry, but in the long run, I was delighted. If he had won, we probably wouldn't have had *Caravans* or *The Source*, both of which were published within the next three years.

Jim didn't lose interest in politics. Several years after his defeat, he served as a Bucks County delegate to the constitutional convention called by the governor of Pennsylvania to rewrite the state constitution. Jim was elected secretary and attended all the sessions; he and Mari even moved to Harrisburg, the state capital, for a year so that he could fulfill his duties. In Harrisburg, Jim met Bob Casey, who later served two terms as governor, and their relationship was a great help years later, when I appealed to Casey for $1 million state grant to add a wing to the Michener Art Museum.

Some years later, during the early 1970s, while Jim was writing *Centennial,* he announced at the start of one of our regular Tuesday drives that he needed to go to Lancaster, in south-central Pennsylvania, to do some research. As we motored along, Jim told us that Lancaster was a jumping-off point for westward-bound covered wagons heading across the continent. That made this little Pennsylvania town an important part of his book.

In Lancaster, we stopped first at the Landis Museum, a "living museum" with restored buildings in which people— all dressed in authentic period clothing—were stitching quilts, weaving, and making copper pots using techniques that were employed at the time the Conestoga wagons headed west. We joined a group tour in progress as the guide explained that covered wagons were generally stained with a mixture of buttermilk and indigo to protect the wood against the weather.

When the tour was over, I stepped up to the guide:

"You see that guy over there?" I asked, pointing to Jim. "That's Jim Michener."

The guide walked over to Jim and looked him straight in the eye. I thought he was going to ask for an autograph. Instead, he said, "Hey, Michener, aren't you the guy that ran for Congress and lost?"

Often, when hot political news broke, Jim was away from home. I don't remember where he was when Watergate was brewing, but it captured his full attention. First, Les Trauch and I and other friends received the following letter:

3 May 73

Dear Herman, Les, Joe, Bill, Pat, Ham
and intellectual wives:

I do wish I could be home to talk politics with someone, because I am prepared to speak for forty-five minutes on any of the following theses, which, taken altogether represent my views on Watergate.

1. The bugging of the headquarters of the Democrats was a silly gesture which should have been cleared up within six days.

2. The attempted cover-up was illegal and has criminal implications.

3. The most serious aspect of the case was the planned attempt to corrupt the inner workings of the opposition party. This is pure corruption of the system.

4. As a [Democratic presidential candidate Edmund S.] Muskie worker, I am appalled to find that it was the Republicans who defeated him with forged documents, so as to ensure the nomination of a weaker candidate.

5. I consider the forging of State Department documents to prove that JFK assassinated [South Vietnam President Ngo Dinh] Diem deplorable.

6. I suspect that Martha [Mrs. John] Mitchell was right all along and thought so from the beginning.

7. It is inconceivable to me that [Attorney General] John Mitchell would, after a totally improper suggestion was made in his presence, allow the same men to come back at him two more times with improved plans to do a totally illegal thing, and to discuss it with him when he was the nation's chief legal officer.

8. Like almost everyone else, I am more than pleased to see [presidential assistants] [John D.] Erlichman and [H. R.] Haldeman depart. They were soulless technocrats, totally unqualified to direct the

social legislation of this country. No Democrat has said anything half so cruel against these two as have their Republican friends. From what I know of the two, only half the truth has been told. We should all rejoice at their departure.

9. I was sorry to see [Attorney General Richard] Kleindienst go. He seemed a pretty good man.

10. No one was sorry to see [presidential counsel John W.] Dean go. He was an arrogant second-rater.

11. Leonard Garment, who replaced him, is a fine man, one to be trusted.

12. It is really gruesome to think that it was this group of men who were leading the attack on the freedom of the press and television. Both the press and the television people need review from time to time, but not dictation from men like this.

13. I agree totally with William Shannon of the New York Times who says that this scandal, which in its simplest outlines, doesn't look bad at all, was generic in the kind of people Mr. Nixon had assembled about him.

14. I have been traveling a good deal in the west, and out here nobody takes the affair very seriously.

15. In Illinois, it ranked eighth in importance behind meat prices, abortion, and busing. By and large, it is an eastern phenomenon, plus all the people elsewhere who worry about good government.

16. Almost every acquaintance I have in these parts dismisses the affair as merely a Democratic-Republican tiff of little consequence.* All believe President

Nixon told the whole truth on television. All believe the whole thing should now be forgotten, and that normal business should be resumed.

17. But none of the professional politicians believe this, and some of the most serious criticism comes from Republicans who feel their jobs in jeopardy in 1974.

18. I am against talk of impeachment. I am against it. I am against it. I have no judgment whether the President told the truth or not. (I thought the last part of his speech appalling.) **. . . .

Jim

* Since then, we've met a few who differ from this.
** MM does not agree.

Jim was fascinated and horrified by the ever-worsening revelations that came out of Watergate. A few months later, he enclosed a thirty-page analysis with this cover letter:

550 East Twelfth

Denver 80203

21 July 1973

Dear Leslie and Herman-Annie,

Herewith the complete version of the Watergate text. In view of the fact that it was written during the first week of June, long before even Dean's testimony, it stands remarkably well as a prediction of what the general mood was going to be.

Will Leslie please forward the text and this letter to Herman Silverman, Old Danboro Road, Doylestown, Penna.

Events of the last few days, and assuming that Nixon will refuse to release the tapes, make me think that we may be heading for a real and perhaps even terrible crisis in which he will endeavor to bull this whole thing through, bring back Haldeman and Ehrlichman, and present us with a semi-dictatorship.

The time may well be at hand when all of us will have to step forward and state explicitly what we will allow and not allow.

I speak from an apprehension growing out of my 70–30 analysis. In the past week I have seen many signs that the 70 see a chance to gain their way, discipline the press, muzzle television, and silence once and for all the critical 30. Criticism coming my way from the 70 is really frightening; support from the 30 is greater than I might have expected. And so we careen along toward confrontation.

The fiasco over the telephone hoax was quite serious, in that it allows the foolish ones to decry Watergate, as Nixon did in his extraordinary 'Let those who will, wallow in Watergate.' I hope you know sensible people who are looking somewhat beyond that. I know some, and they seem quite stalwart. We may need them.

In the analysis which he enclosed, Jim predicted three possibilities: impeachment, resignation, or Nixon "toughing it out." Jim thought that if Nixon did tough it out, "precautions" should be taken to limit his powers to appoint judges to the U.S. Supreme Court, to conduct foreign affairs, and to declare war.

As usual, Jim's thinking was perceptive, as this short excerpt from his long analysis shows:

> One intellectual loss I regret. Just when a group of conservative philosophers and writers were beginning to build a new establishment to challenge the old-style liberal one, Watergate knocks their pretensions flat, proving that what liberals had been claiming all along was true. Watergate is a typical right-wing debacle. When liberals misuse a government they do so by means of theft, nepotism and stupendous bureaucracies. (Can anyone imagine a bunch of Democrats in charge of $60,000,000 without someone trying to steal half of it?) The classic right-wing abuses are less flamboyant but more dangerous: assaults on individual freedom, corruption of power processes, flagrant disregard for human rights. Philosophers of the oft-proclaimed New Republican Majority like Irving Kristol, Levin Philips, William Buckley, Patrick Buchanan and Jeffrey Hart should address themselves to this phenomenon, so that when conservatism wins its next overwhelming victory it can avoid the disasters of this one.
>
> One casualty we can all deplore. The proposed Bicentennial birthday celebration will probably have

to be cancelled, for it would be difficult for President Nixon to come before the public with . . . speeches inviting the nation to join him in celebrating freedom. 1976, which should have been a glorious culmination of his eight years in power, will be a time of relieved dismissal. Any grandiose plans for jubilation should be scrapped.

It is always possible that new revelations may force the House to vote a reluctant bill of impeachment, but I hope not. Or the day could come when senior Republican senators will troop into the White House solemn-faced to announce, "Sir, you are damaging the nation and the party, and you must resign. If you refuse, we shall desert you." If either of these events does occur, I have confidence that our republic will survive, as it has withstood so many other traumas during the exciting years I have been watching it.

What made politics so interesting to all of us, as Jim summed up so well in his letters, was our feeling that what happened in government made a difference in the lives of every American. Politics mattered, and not just in elections— they were a factor, we believed, in so many of the social issues of the day.

One of our more lively discussions took place during the autumn of 1992, when Jim and Mari and Ann and I drove from Maine to Quebec. Jim mentioned an interview with a Texas newspaper reporter who had asked him who, in all the world, he would like to eat dinner with if he had the chance.

"I told them Jean Harris," Jim said.

*Newlyweds—Vange and Jim in New York City
in September, 1948, shortly after their marriage*

Launching South Pacific—*Richard Rodgers, Oscar Hammerstein II, Mary Martin, and James Michener in a 1949 publicity photo*

Mari and Jim at their wedding in Chicago, October 23, 1955

Campaigning hard for Congress, Jim ran as a Democrat in Pennsylvania's 8th District.

YOU'LL BE PROUD
OF
James A. MICHENER
IN
CONGRESS

VOTE DEMOCRATIC
NOV. 6, 1962
"Elect A National Figure to Serve You In Washington"

Always gracious, Jim signed copies of Centennial *at Farley's Bookshop in New Hope, Pennsylvania, in 1974.*

Above, from left—On a visit to the Everglades in April, 1988, Herman, Ann, Mari, and Jim were photographed by a retired sailor who had joined the Navy after reading Tales of the South Pacific.

At right—Mari Michener in 1974

Gradually, with the support of Jim and Mari Michener, the century-old Bucks County Prison in Doylestown, above, was converted into the James A. Michener Art Museum. This building now houses the museum's administrative offices.

Top left—At the ground-breaking of the museum's first expansion in 1992, Jim toured the site with architect Lynn Taylor.

Top right—The main entrance to the Michener Museum.

At the age of 85, Jim revisited eight of his boyhood homes in Doylestown, posing for this photograph in a borrowed jacket.

The three of us were astonished. "Oh Jim! No!" said Mari. Jean Harris, former headmistress of the Madeira School, a prestigious girls' school, had been convicted in 1980 of killing her longtime lover, Dr. Herman Tarnower, creator of the Scarsdale Diet. Jealous that Tarnower was seeing another woman, Harris confronted him at his home, where they wrestled over a gun and he was shot. Despite her upstanding background and evidence that Tarnower taunted her with his infidelities, she was sentenced to life in prison.

"Jim," I said, "I don't understand; her name hasn't even been in the papers for years. She's in jail."

Jim took an unusual view: "She's a political prisoner," he said. "There isn't a governor of New York who has had the guts to give her a pardon, and there's no reason for her to have been in jail this long.

"It's all politics; the governors are afraid if they pardon her, it might send a signal they're soft on crime. In France the murder would have been understood as a 'crime of passion' and the life sentence would never have been imposed."

Jim never did dine with Jean Harris, but New York Governor Mario Cuomo later did have the courage to grant her clemency and release her after she had served twelve years in prison.

On the rare occasions when Jim and Mari entertained, they brought together others who enjoyed talking about international politics. In October, 1980, Jim threw a two-day surprise party to celebrate his and Mari's twenty-fifth wedding anniversary and invited about thirty of their friends from all over the country to St. Michaels, Maryland.

At Jim's expense, we all checked into a beautiful old hotel

in Easton, The Tidewater Inn. To celebrate the occasion, Jim had flown in orchid leis from Hawaii.

That evening, Ann and I were lucky enough to be seated with CBS Nightly News anchor Walter Cronkite and his wife, Betsy, who had sailed their boat up to St. Michaels from Annapolis. Our conversation was mostly about Israel, and Cronkite said that he believed the Israelis were foolish to try to hold on to the West Bank. His comment disturbed me. I didn't know a lot about the ins and outs of what was happening in Israel, but I did know that the West Bank was only about ten miles from Tel Aviv and about three miles from Jerusalem.

"You say your boat is berthed in St. Michaels?" I asked.

"That's right," said Cronkite.

"About ten miles away from here," I noted.

"That's right," he repeated.

"Well, how would you like it if you had an enemy sitting here with their guns pointing at your boat just ten miles away? That's how Israel must feel every time someone suggests they allow the Arabs only a few miles from their major cities."

We had quite a discussion, but I don't think I persuaded him.

Maybe we were naive, but Jim and I believed that our elected leaders should care as strongly as we did about these issues—and not just about whether they were going to win the next election. Over the years, Jim became pretty savvy about the strategies of national politics, as this letter about the 1988 presidential campaign shows:

21 April 1988

Dear Anne and Herman,

I promised I'd write after the New York primary and thoughts that have generated since then follow.

1. [Michael] Dukakis did better than I expected. [Al] Gore did much worse. And [Jesse] Jackson a little worse.

2. This puts Dukakis in a better position than I had expected him to be at this time.

3. I see much comment on the fact that Jackson will have to be the vice-presidential candidate.

4. I remain convinced that if Jackson were to be the candidate for president, the state vote would be 50–0, with Jackson getting Washington, D.C.

5. I have always been afraid that if Jackson were even the v-p candidate the Democrats would be doomed, but not by so wide a margin. They still might lose in states 50–0 but each race would be closer.

6. My real fear is that the Demos might lose the Senate and maybe even effective control of the House, and this must be guarded against. It's a danger if there is a wild landslide Republican victory.

7. I believe I would work to help a Dukakis-Jackson victory, would not speak out against it, but would expect to lose the election.

8. But in the event #7 occurred, I would expect a new kind of Democratic party that would win in 1992. But the old crystal ball is cloudy.

Jim

Until the end of his life, Jim remained interested in politics. In 1992, as the Bush administration was coming to a close, he was ready for a change. On October 19, he wrote a letter from his home in Austin to Democratic leader Milton Berkes to support Bucks County congressman Pete Kostmayer, who was in a tough race for reelection.

> I go to bed each night praying: 'Let the good news continue!' and I walk around each day with my fingers crossed. Fifteen more days, come the return of decency. I'm shocked at the way the Bush Administration is unraveling; those men should be ashamed. To help our side you may release the following:
>
> 'I am voting for Peter Kostmayer because he has proved to be a fine representative of Bucks County interests in Congress, because he is a knowledgeable student of political conditions, and because he is a thoroughly honorable citizen, both in politics and in private life.
>
> He has served our district with distinction and enjoys a fine reputation in Washington. He is worth keeping in office to continue the good work he's been doing.'

Jim's luck didn't change, though; despite Jim's support, Kostmayer lost.

As I look back at these letters now, and realize how completely Jim's politics changed over the years, I have to chuckle. Ann and I remember well sitting in our living room with Jim and Vange in November, 1952, the night Adlai

Stevenson lost the presidential election to Eisenhower. Ann, Vange, and I were so depressed—Vange was in tears. But Jim couldn't have been more pleased; at that time, he was a staunch Republican and had voted against Stevenson. I like to think that our conversations on our long drives through the countryside during the years that followed had something to do with his conversion.

10. The Aqua Club

*I*t was during the early years of our friendship, in 1955, when Jim and I embarked on an adventure together: we decided to build a swim club and nightclub.

During this time Jim was staying at my house quite a lot between writing trips. By then my landscape business had become a swimming pool business; I had started a company which I called Sylvan Pools, and Jim had bought a one-third interest in the company. Swimming clubs were becoming a big thing; I had built several, and I told Jim that I thought we could make some money if we built a swim club. So we formed a partnership and, for $10,000, we bought ten acres in Bucks County, just south of New Hope along Route 202 in Solebury. We decided to call our enterprise The Aqua Club.

Originally, the club was supposed to be very rustic, a place for picnics and possibly business gatherings. But for some reason, we felt we could be even more successful by adding an adjacent restaurant and a nightclub, which we called The Fountainhead.

For the next few years, building The Aqua Club and then The Fountainhead took a lot of our attention and conversation. We were both enthusiastic about its prospects. Here's part of a letter Jim sent from Tokyo to me and to our friend, William Viterelli, who was working for me:

March 14, 1955

Dear Herman and Vit,

The plans for the club look excellent. I like the idea of lots of space, lots of woods, and an area in which to grow. . . .

Herman, your plan for memberships is very wise and should yield the maximum take. There is a slightly unfortunate tinge to the members being required to shell out fees each time they attend, but I'm sure you'll be able to explain that away to them. Certainly, I think you were extraordinarily bright in working out the tax angle the way you did, and I'm sure you're on the right path. Makes the fees sound much lower, makes the deal a better one all the way around.

As to finances, I enclose a carbon of a letter I'm sending off today, the original to the bank, the copy to [my secretary] Mrs. Shoemaker, the second copy to you. As I understand it, there should be enough money in the Hilltop account to provide the money you need. If anything goes wrong, let me know as per the addresses on the attached carbon. I am increasingly happy with this investment and increasingly sure that you and Vit will come up with the right ideas for making everything practical. I only wish I could be there with you during the formative stages. But my participation can come later.

If the cost goes way beyond estimate, I think we should mortgage it to the hilt with whatever bank seems interested. In our party was a brilliant real estate operator from West Virginia. We talked long hours about similar problems that arose in his business. He says he would make the banks carry the whole load, if he could, for he feels that the only way a young man can make money is on bank's money. Like everyone else, he feels that an enterprise should have a solid home base on which he almost never borrows (in his case a lumber yard) and he told me of several instances in which he quickly got out of deals that were going to imperil his basic financial position. But on his chance-taking deals he has often constructed pyramids so intricate that even he doesn't always understand them. He said that if he were your partner he would get as many clubs operating as possible and expect to lose one or two of them in the fortunes of war (the banks taking them over) but he would expect to gain enough on those he was able to hold onto to make an over-all killing. He was very emphatic.

So in accordance with all everyone has told me, I'd rely upon bank funds wherever possible. I'll try to keep some money around to float new enterprises, for I strongly believe in this venture.

I also like the businessmen's assembly area, since it could probably be projected without too much additional expense. If the idea looks feasible, and if you think there are enough businesses that would be interested (how about company picnics on off days) why go ahead without bothering to check with me again. I trust your judgment and would be glad to see whatever money we might make reinvested so that the company sheet shows a loss at the end of the year. . . .

Mich

Despite our enthusiasm, The Fountainhead was a money pit from the start. Getting a liquor license was an ordeal because Bucks County had a limited allotment of licenses, and development costs were higher than we expected.

Jim and Mari were married later that year and were traveling in Asia, so Jim and I had to conduct a lot of business by mail. As partners in The Aqua Club and The Fountainhead, Jim and I were under a lot of financial pressure, but Jim's letters show that he didn't let it get to him:

New Delhi
January 13, 1956

Dear Herman,

First let me assure you that I will kick in with the $2,400 you suggest for keeping Fountainhead alive during this season. But for the time being I cannot decide how this ought to be done, since I am waiting for several reports on what my finances are at the moment. These should arrive within the week, whereupon I will be able to see where the money can come from. I will also wait till then to send you the $2,000, although that is clearly earmarked. Problem is, I don't know exactly where the money is nor how much, but I'll write promptly as soon as the mail from New York arrives. . . .

Without having the financial figures of my own affairs before me, I can say that I am going to make every effort to apply a real chunk of my income to rescuing the Trenton loan, lest we strike trouble in the stock market. As co-partner in the Aqua Club-Fountainhead business I think we must direct all our efforts to making another sizable chunk of dough, and retiring more of the loan. Then I'd feel better and so would the company! So if you can finagle a real profit from Aqua Club and only a breakeven at Fountainhead, I'd be happy. We should then retire—between my personal income and the Aqua Club profits—at least $50,000, and I'd be willing to leave the other $50,000 ride for a while, which would amount in fact to a mortgage of $90,000, the Doylestown Bank holding the other $40,000.

But Herman, we must be prepared every minute from now on against the possibility that the Doylestown Bank might call their mortgage. I know they said they wouldn't, and I am sure they have no intention of doing so, and I know that Barnes and Fretz entertain good feelings toward us . . . but we don't know what's going to happen either to the bank or to the market. So let's be in a position where we could pay it off or assume it ourselves. One good year of profits, plus my income, could make this possible. That should be our

target: not to pay it off, but to be able to do so if necessary. I'm sure you agree.

I liked the Fountainhead brochures and was
encouraged by your report. The $500 a week for
salaries alone sort of staggers me, but . . . . Glad the
New Years paid off. Let's hope we hit some more.

Warmly,

Jim

A few months after that, we got the liquor license for The
Fountainhead, allowing us to attract the dancing and eating
crowd. We booked Harry Belafonte and other top-flight
entertainers, and we had dancing on the roof in the moon-
light. There was nothing like it in our area; we drew
customers from Philadelphia, Princeton, and even New York.

But it's tough to make money in that business. Jim was
busy writing his books and traveling around the world, and I
was too busy building Sylvan Pools to spend much time at
The Fountainhead. The liquor license didn't improve our
prospects as much as we had hoped. Jim and Mari returned
to the States later that spring, and Ann and I met them in
Chicago. We spent most of the drive back to Pennsylvania
weighing our options.

By August, 1956, we were $100,000 in the hole. Our
lawyer suggested a way out: "Go into legal bankruptcy. Pay
about twenty-two cents on the dollar and start over with a
clean slate."

I didn't have much money, but even so, the idea didn't
appeal to me, and Jim agreed. One evening at his house, Jim
said to me: "Herman, we simply cannot start our careers with

a bankruptcy that would stain our characters. We'd always be known as two adventurers who chiseled their creditors. We'll pay off the debts and put this behind us."

Jim came up with the money. I gave him a note for half, and paid him back at the going rate of interest over ten years. We sold the club and pool at auction. The Fountainhead has since become an attractive restaurant and catering hall for community events and weddings.

Many years later, when I reminded Jim of this episode, he expressed his own feelings on the matter in a letter from Austin dated July 24, 1995:

> You allude to many events we shared, you and I and Annie and Mari, but the one that is burned into my memory came when that project you and I were engaged in turned sour and we faced the probability of having to cough up huge numbers of dollars to clear the financial charges against us. We were advised by many to go into bankruptcy and the temptation was great, for many of the debts were our fault, but after a painful weekend when things were really bleak and it looked as if we liquidated we would still be left with a huge debt that you and I would have to pay. We had a Monday morning meeting to review the disaster and I don't recall who first voiced an opinion, but I do know that when it came my time to speak I said, 'Herman, you and I cannot afford to go into bankruptcy. It's against the grain of our personal lives. I'm convinced that you are destined to be an impor-

tant man in this community and I expect to keep my typewriter working. Let's pay off the debts right now, get this damned thing behind us, and get on with our lives. There are good years ahead.'

You never demurred. You never put forward any weasling way by which we might save our necks. We had the auction. We lost a bundle, and we paid every cent in full. More important, you went on to become one of the richest men in the county. As you said in your letter: 'My children help maintain and manage our 14 big buildings, office buildings, banks, shopping centers.' I'm proud of you Kiddo, and think: 'He could never have done it if he'd destroyed his reputation by going bankrupt.' I, too, have kept my head above water and judge that for every dollar we lost in that failed venture, we got back $100,000. That's the great gamble of life. Really believe that doing the right thing will pay off in the future. I believe that without question.

The two partners in an ill-conceived enterprise had lost a small fortune, yet they remained friends and even entertained subsequent ventures. The experience taught me to keep my eye on the ball and do what I do best.

In retrospect, I wonder what possessed us to think we could make a success of the restaurant business, the toughest business in the world.

11. Money

*J*im's attitude toward money was complicated.

He had no interest in possessions, but he often owned several residences at the same time, some of which he locked up and never set foot in for years at a time. He donated more than one residence to a university or another charitable institution; he offered one house in Doylestown to his cousin, Virginia, and when she declined, gave it to Pearl Buck's foundation *and* sent a check for its value to Virginia.

Throughout his life, he remained personally frugal. We were both nearly broke when we first met in 1947. Once or twice a year, we used to go to a men's clothing store on Callowhill Street in Philadelphia where we could buy clothes at about one-third the retail price. Jim developed a long-standing friendship with the store proprietor, whom we called "Handsome Harry," and he continued to buy most of his clothes there for years, even after he became rich.

Jim seemed to have trouble understanding the extent of his wealth, relative to most people's income. One day he asked me, "What does a secretary make, what does a conductor make? How much money does a person have to have to live the life we live?" I told him, "Between a quarter-million and a half-million in annual income."

Jim never kept money in his pocket. Mari would pay—occasionally. On our bigger trips together, I would pay and keep track of the expenses, then drop Mari a note about the total. After one trip in 1992, I waited so long for repayment that I finally had to write to their New York accountant.

Sometimes, Jim could be downright cheap. Once during the 1980s, when he was a multimillionaire, and long after he had run for Congress, I called him to ask for a donation to the re-election campaign of Pennsylvania Rep. Pete Kostmayer, a congressman he cared about. He said, "Give him $50 in my name."

When I protested and told him, "Jim, that's not enough," he said, "Okay, make it $100." (I think Mari was tighter with a dollar than Jim. Yet, wherever they traveled, she shopped. She bought *crates* of stuff. When their houses were cleaned out after her death, there were crates and crates and crates—many of them never opened.)

Jim never stopped being amused at how other people spent their money. In March, 1984, he wrote to me from Austin about the results of a charity auction that included some of his books:

> Last night, at a whing-ding Texas auction, a set of six of my novels, properly autographed, sold for $21,000. I said $21,000.
>
> It happened this way. Spirited bidding carried the six books to $7,000, at which they were knocked down. But then a man in the audience shouted: "At that price I'll take a set, too." Whereupon another man shouted: "Count me in, too." So the deal was struck.

Now that we know the market exists out there, I hope these facts will be taken into account at the pricing of my future books.

Before he died, Jim gave away most of his possessions. Published reports say that he contributed more than $117 million to various causes and institutions. His art and literary endowments to the University of Texas at Austin were reportedly worth more than $64 million, and I can vouch for the fact that Jim and Mari donated $8.5 million to the James A. Michener Art Museum in Doylestown.

As a child, Jim lived in nine different houses in Doylestown. Jim told me that they moved so often that one day he asked his mother, "What's the matter? Don't we ever pay our rent?" Eventually he learned that a local real estate agent let his mother move her family into vacant houses the agent had listed; he felt they might sell faster if they were occupied. Of course, once they sold, the Micheners had to move on.

Many years later, in 1992, when Jim was back for a visit, he said, "I want a picture of myself in front of every house I ever lived in." We had a hell of job getting a photographer that day. I got four or five of my jackets so that Jim wouldn't be wearing the same thing in every picture. He sat on the porch of the front steps of eight different houses—all but one were still standing, and he had his picture taken there on empty ground.

I grew up poor, too. We paid $8 a month to rent the third floor of a Philadelphia rowhouse that had just one bathroom. But unlike Jim, who never bonded with the foster children in his household, my two brothers and I formed a strong family unit with my mother.

Both Jim and I were raised without fathers. Jim never knew who his father was. My own father died when I was nine years old, and I remember nothing about him at all. I know that he was a paperhanger and that when he came home at night, he played the mandolin. I only know that because I have a picture of him dressed in a Cossack costume, playing the instrument.

Once, early in our friendship, while Jim and I were taking a walk, we discussed the effects of not having had fathers when we were growing up. Jim considered it not without its advantages, because he had been able to come and go as he pleased, with no father always looking after him or holding him accountable. Although he'd had no dad to take him fishing or to ball games, he was able to travel on his own, and at the age of thirteen he began hitchhiking all over the United States. After my father died, I was pretty much on my own, too; my mother had two other boys to look after while trying to earn a living as the country headed into the Great Depression. I didn't have to worry about whether my father was someone I would have to emulate, or be ashamed of. I was free as a bird. I wasn't forced to practice a religion, and nobody told me what to do—my mother told me simply, "Don't do anything that would make me embarrassed."

But I didn't grow up with the fear of being poor that Jim had all his life. After I sold Sylvan Pools in 1971, I went into business for myself again, developing commercial properties. I enjoy the risks as part of the process of doing business.

When people say to me, "What do you do for a hobby?" I say, "I think about making money." I've made or raised a lot of money in my life—for public housing as a member of the board of Pennsylvania's Housing Finance Agency, for our local hospital in Doylestown, for the Michener Museum, and for other organizations. Those are the things I'm interested in—my family, my community, and making money. I've always been that way.

When I was very young, there was a camp for poor kids like me called S.G.F. in Collegeville, Pennsylvania. We spent two weeks out in the country. When camp was over, we lined up in front of our bunks and a guy pulled up in a car and handed each camper a book, a different book for each kid. He saw me waiting in line and said, "You look like a guy who's interested in money," and gave me a book of Horatio Alger stories. I read every one of those books. I took their message seriously—if you work hard, are good to your mother, and are honest, you can make it.

In his last years, Jim wrote a marvelous little book about Spain called *Miracle in Seville,* which was published in 1995. I said to him, "Jim, you haven't been in Spain for twenty-five years, and yet you write this like you were there yesterday, it's so vivid. How do you do that?" And he said to me, "Herman, that's what I *do*. If you want to be a good writer, you have to have a good memory."

Making money—that's what *I* do. It has its risks, but it's a lot of fun.

After the Aqua Club fiasco, we had some pretty hard times at Sylvan Pools. I had taken a lot of capital out of the company and put it into the swim club and The Fountainhead. We asked Jim to lend us some money for Sylvan Pools, but I think his accountant advised him against it. (Since then, I tell people who come to me for advice, "Never listen to your

accountant or your lawyer when it comes to business, because they're always trying to protect you.") So instead of
getting the money from Jim, we borrowed from one of our
bankers—who shouldn't have lent us the money, because we
weren't credit-worthy at the time.

In 1959, after Sylvan Pools was on firm footing, I bought
back Jim's one-third interest in the business and gave it to
my younger brother, Ira. We built it into a national company
and eventually sold it for a handsome profit. I think Jim
respected me because he knew I took that business through
many hard times when even *he* didn't want to lend me money.

One of Jim's few personal indulgences was his art collection. Long before they became popular, he concentrated on
buying Japanese woodblock prints. In fact, he became an
expert; his book, *The Floating World*, was one of the first to
introduce the western world to the art form, and he later
wrote three more books on the subject. He used to say, in all
seriousness, that by educating the rest of the world about
Japanese prints, he had managed to price himself right out of
the market.

"Herman," he told me, "I used to pay $50 to $75 a print,
and now they're $250 to $500. I told the dealer, 'Hey, just three
or four years ago I was paying you $50 each.' The guy replied,
'Yes, but since you wrote those books on Japanese prints,
everybody wants to buy the things, and the price has tripled.'
There it is; I cut my own throat by writing those books."

One day, Jim got a phone call from a stranger who asked,
"Are you the author of *The Floating World*?" When Jim said
yes, the caller told him that he wanted advice about some
Japanese prints he'd inherited from his father: "We want to

sell, but we don't know what they're worth. I've got three sisters dying to get their hands on cash. My father didn't leave us much, but we think the prints are valuable. Is there any way you can tell us what they're worth?"

Jim agreed to try to help and told him, "If you can send me a list of what you've got, with some slides or pictures, I could give you an idea of what they're worth. I'd have a better idea if I could see them."

After he got a look at the prints, Jim gave the man names of potential buyers and told him: "You can tell whoever buys them that I'll testify to their value, and it's quite large. Get in touch with these people; they're in the market and will probably want to buy." Jim's estimate was about $100,000.

Three years passed, and the man called again. He told Jim that he never had gotten in touch with the buyers Jim recommended, but that now he was down on his luck and had to have cash. Because he felt that Jim had leveled with him, he wanted to sell to Jim.

Jim protested, "I can't pay what I said they're worth. I don't have that kind of money." He really didn't, at that stage in his career.

"Well," the man countered, "could you give us $75,000?"

"I could do that over a three-year period," Jim replied.

The man refused. "No, we need the cash now, on the barrel-head."

Jim went to New York and took out a loan. He added the prints to his own considerable collection, and years later, when he donated thousands of Japanese prints to the Honolulu Academy of Arts, the collection was valued at about $20 million.

In later years, Jim and Mari collected modern art. Before they began buying, they decided to buy only the works of artists who had lived and worked during their own lifetimes. As he had with Japanese prints, Jim researched the artists whose work interested him. He and Mari read books on various schools of art and sought advice from dealers and other experts. Mari had a good eye for art, too; they were both knowledgeable collectors and investors, and they usually agreed on their acquisitions.

When it came to buying art, Jim was true to his spirit of adventure and his sense of honor. If he and Mari saw a painting that they thought showed talent but which they didn't particularly care for, they often visited the studio and bought another painting directly from the artist. But they always paid a commission to the gallery representing the artist.

Jim and Mari built a large addition to their home in Bucks County to house their paintings. They were hung on sliding boards that could be pulled out so that all the paintings— about 300—could be viewed in that room. However, I can't remember anyone ever going up to look at them.

Except for their house on the hill in Bucks County, there was never any artwork on the walls in all the homes where Ann and I visited Jim and Mari—none at all—with one exception. In the 1960s, Jim began making collages, some of them quite elaborate. Several of these hung in Jim and Mari's various homes.

In June, 1966, Jim wrote asking me to mail him postcards when Ann and I traveled around the world. He was making a collage featuring stamps and wanted his friends to mail cards with "as many different cheap colored stamps as possible," pasted on according to his instructions: "Mail the cards of course, standard mail. The more beat up they look when I get them in Pipersville, the better for my purpose."

Jim later donated his collection of modern art to the University of Texas, and I've heard that the collection was appraised at more than $17 million when the donation was made. Even so, Jim always said that about one-third of the works in his collection were of little value; he told me that he and Mari couldn't always afford to buy top of the line, and that they never paid more than $5,000 for a painting.

Although most of these paintings were sent to Austin, ten paintings remained in Bucks County through an arrangement that came about almost casually.

Mari and Jim were wintering in Coral Gables in 1988, and I was checking their Bucks County house periodically. In one of our telephone conversations, I told Jim that some of his paintings were beginning to mildew—including paintings by Helen Frankenthaler, Grace Hartigan, Lee Gatch, and Norman Bluhm.

"There's no humidity or temperature control in the house," I said. "I think those paintings should be taken out of there." Then I added what was in the back of my mind: "Why don't you donate them to the museum?"

In fact, there *was* no museum at that time, though one was in the works. We were just beginning to convert the abandoned, century-old Bucks County Jail on Pine Street in Doylestown to the Michener Museum. But Jim agreed: "Okay. Go ahead and take them."

I knew Mari well enough to know that she would want to have a say in the matter, so I asked Jim to have her call me.

Jim would give away anything, but Mari was just the opposite. And she usually had the final say.

Sure enough, Mari returned my call with the announcement that the paintings were already part of the Micheners' gift to the University of Texas. "But you can have them on permanent loan," she said.

To make sure everything was aboveboard, I asked Mari to fly up to Bucks County. "I can't take the paintings out of your house unless you're here," I told her. "Somebody has to be a witness, because they're very valuable paintings, probably worth more than two million dollars."

She agreed, and when she arrived, I rented a U-Haul, rounded up a couple of strong helpers, and we moved the paintings to a museum which was generous enough to store them while the Michener Museum was being built.

While moving the paintings, we noticed a large, unopened crate about six feet by eight feet. Using a crowbar and hammer, we pried it open—to reveal a painting attributed to the internationally respected abstract expressionist Franz Kline. That painting, too, is now displayed at the Michener Museum.

Odd as it seems for someone who didn't care to own anything, Jim had several homes toward the end of his life, none of them luxurious or pretentious. He and Mari always chose a place based on the locale of Jim's next book, or on considerations of climate. When he was writing *Chesapeake*, he bought a home on the Eastern Shore of Maryland; their condo in Florida was home during *Caribbean*, and for *Texas*, he bought a house in Austin. They always chose something modest.

Even after Jim finished *Caribbean*, he and Mari liked to live in Florida in the winter. Eventually, they bought into a retirement complex in St. Petersburg on the grounds of Eckerd College, where Jim was a visiting professor of writing. Jim liked the place because it included a hospital, a nursing wing, and long-term care facilities. Another advantage was the community dining room, where Jim and Mari could have all their meals. They purchased two condos and combined them, so Jim and Mari could each have an office—Jim's for writing (and Mari's to let the mail pile up).

Their final, permanent home was in Austin. Late in 1984, as Jim was completing the manuscript for *Texas*, he was offered a professorship at the university's writer-in-residence program, and they decided to buy a small house there.

The next year, Jim sent Christmas greetings to several of us in a funny letter dated December 20, 1985. As usual, he pounded out this long letter on one of the typewriters he kept at each of his houses, this time using a capital S and striking it by hand to form a dollar sign:

> We were invited to a great bull sale at a posh ranch near here and the day before they sent their plane for us—how else?—I read by accident that the owner had settled his claim with the other contestants for $86,000,000 (Imagine having a typewriter in Texas that has no $ sign!). . . He picked up a neat million on the sale, so in celebration gave a dinner party for 600 of his intimate friends, then a lunch for 900 of the buyers, and an apres-dinner for 700. Highlight of sale came when the auctioneer stopped the bidding and said: "I'm afraid we have a husband bidding against

his wife down here." Lights flashed on the pair and he cried: "Good God! What are you doing?" And she cried: "You dumb ox, you can't even remember your own signals." Then everybody including the couple burst into laughter, even though the misunderstanding had cost them about $6,000 extra dollars. . . .

Football is not king here; it is the deity, especially in high school. To take notes I went to last Friday night's playoff between Austin and San Antonio high schools and the latter school, Churchill, could have beaten most of the small Pennsylvania colleges. Squad of about 90 giants. Coaching staff—now are you ready for this—ten! . . . Drill squad of pretty girls in uniform, about 116. Thirty cheer leaders. Three superb baton twirlers. And little girls' platoon to run errands between the various parts. Man sitting next to me said: "Who's playing? Wife and I drove eighty miles to see this. Our team was eliminated last Friday night, but a guy has to do something on Fridays." He asked me what the name of the San Antonio team was and I told him Churchill. "What's the W for on the band uniforms?" and I said, "I suppose it's for Winston Churchill," and he stared at me in disbelief: "You mean a self respecting Texas high school is named after a European? Next thing you know we'll have Adolf Hitler High. If it's from San Antone, it ought to call itself Enchilada High."

After they settled in Austin, Jim and Mari moved several times. Earlier they had rented a little ranch house at 3506

Mount Bonnell Road, a few miles from the university. I suggested to Mari that they buy a house in a nearby neighborhood with rolling landscape and beautiful views. But she told me that Jim, who liked to walk in the evenings, wouldn't be able to navigate the hills. They then bought a one-story ranch house on Mountain Laurel Lane, but it proved to be too small, and after two years they bought another, slightly larger, one-story ranch house around the corner at 2719 Mountain Laurel Lane.

However, summer in Texas, Jim said, is "hell," so in 1990, he and Mari decided to get a summer place in Maine. They found a nice condominium in a new development in Brunswick, near Bowdoin College.

Their condo in Brunswick was at 29 Starwell Lane and was what we in the East call a twin house and elsewhere is called a duplex. It was about as luxurious as anywhere Jim and Mari had ever lived, except for their home in Bucks County, but nobody would think it was the home of a millionaire.

The development was located in a wooded tract, and the developer had gone broke three-quarters of the way through the project, leaving a five-acre parcel of empty land right next to Jim's house which was becoming a dump for construction refuse. Jim and Mari were powerless to get anyone to clean up the empty site, so Jim put in a low bid with the bank and was delighted when the bank accepted:

> First thing I did was call in a guy with ten bulldozers and machines to turn the junk pile into a park, and gave him extra to plant 35 good sized evergreens. The bank screamed: "You can't do that until the papers are

signed," and I said: "We just did it." Then I was terri-
fied that we had made the place so beautiful that
they'd find cause to cancel the deal, but a lawyer whis-
pered, "Jim, the bank has more than fifty deals like
this. If you raised hell, they'd give you the land, to get
rid of it."

Years later, Jim offered to sell the park to the other
landowners, but they wanted him to donate it instead. He
eventually sold it to a developer.

By this time, Jim and Mari hadn't used the house in Bucks
County for years; a series of house sitters stayed in the house,
and Jim and Mari stayed with us on their rare trips to Pennsylvania. In the early 1990s, Mari phoned from Texas,
agonizing about the property. The people who had been living there were about to retire and move out.

"We must have somebody living there," Mari said. "It's
very isolated and we're afraid it may be vandalized."

"Why do you keep it?" I asked her. "Why don't you give it
to Delaware Valley College in Doylestown? You don't need it."

Mari wasn't one to turn loose of an asset that easily. "Let
me talk to Jim," she said.

Jim liked the idea of giving away the house, but he wanted
to maintain his Pennsylvania residency for voting purposes. I
suggested they keep lifetime rights to the house, which they
did. Jim wasn't interested in a shrine to his memory, and after
Mari died, he gave the school permission to either use the
house or sell it. Mari never did approve of giving away that
house; Jim said that it was because during her own childhood, she didn't have a secure, permanent home.

Even late in life, Jim was afraid of being cheated out of his money, or having Mari cheated out of it after his death. In the back of his mind, he was always afraid that he would end up in the poorhouse like the unfortunate people his aunt used to take in. At least twice, he was asked for financial assistance by important figures in his life—his former literary agent and, later, one of his many secretaries. In the first case, he gave grudgingly; in the other, he flatly refused.

Despite Jim's natural generosity, the conflict with his secretary was one which I don't understand to this day. To protect her privacy, I'm going to call her "Barbara" and her husband "Joe." Barbara had worked for Jim for several years in the late 1970s at a modest wage that didn't equal her value. In 1979 her marriage was coming to an end, and she desperately needed temporary financial help. She asked me to approach Jim for a loan. Jim was living in St. Michaels at the time, and we corresponded about Barbara's problem:

May 22, 1979

Hi Jim:

I spoke to Barbara today. No doubt about it, she must divorce Joe. No other alternative to this is possible as far as she is concerned.

This, of course, will change her income and create a problem for her unless her income improves over what it is now.

As a bare minimum, she will need $200.00 per week. Out of this she will have to pay for Blue Cross and Blue Shield since she will lose the coverage she has now from Joe's job. She will also have to pay Social Security so the $200.00 a week is tight. She feels that as a single parent her [child] could get a grant or scholarship. . . .

Her idea to sell off a two acre parcel is a good one. She needs some cash now to settle some bills that have piled up and to see her through this period of divorce.

Jim, she needs a one shot loan of about $5,000.00 to be paid back with interest (about 9%), when she sells the parcel, which could be in the next six months.

Jim, I had a good talk with Barbara. She is now in a much better frame of mind than when we spoke last. She loves working for you and wants to continue. If you can see your way clear to help her out at this time it would be great for her and you would be doing her a real good deed.

I told her I would write to you about her needs and problem so she is aware of our communication. Maybe you should talk to her as soon as you get a chance.

If I can be of any further help, please let me know.

Herman

A week later, Jim replied:

St. Michaels, Maryland
29 May 1979

Dear Herman,

You may discuss this letter with Barbara and show it to her if that seems best.

In dealing with her problem I am confronted by a strong legal tradition which says that if an outsider interferes in any way in a marital situation, he may be subject to a law suit and rather heavy penalties for alienating affections. For that reason, I refused to give Barbara any advice when she talked to me and would refuse to do so were she to talk [to me] again. I suggested strongly that she consult with her minister, who would not be under the restraints which inhibit me.

It would be dreadfully wrong for me, her employer, to advise her what to do in her situation, and it would be insane for me to advance her the money against her wages to enable her to get a divorce. In fact, as she knows, it was my strong advice—guided by my belief that her first requirement is to ensure her economic base for the next twenty-five years—that she work things out with Joe, stay married to him, and ask for outside counseling from her minister or other legally qualified person.

I am perhaps too concerned about the financial security of people in their fifties, but if so I can be excused because I meet so many who have made wrong choices which have imperiled their careers and who now have to seek help. I have never taken money very seriously except when people come to me and say they will commit suicide if I don't find them some. I cannot be either a counselor or an aide in helping Barbara to imperil her financial position.

Therefore I simply cannot advance her the $5,000 she says she needs for a divorce. To do so would be legally and morally wrong. I think that she ought to stay married.

But if this becomes impossible, and if on her own she decides that she cannot abide her present situation, and if she settles the problem within her own perimeters, I would be eager to retain her friendship; and I would consider a loan at any time, for she is a dear, good person for whom I feel sympathy and affection.

When my former secretary, Evelyn Shoemaker, came to the end of her working days Mari and I provided her with an apartment in Hawaii for the rest of her life, so we are not indifferent to the people who have worked for us. Should Barbara decide on her own to get a divorce, we would of course want to continue our relationship with her; and there are many directions in which this could go.

But to encourage and finance a divorce is simply out of the question. We deem it unwise for her and illegal for us. She has a fine [child] and a husband who has been congenial, and I think she ought to consider carefully before breaking loose. I have seen too many women do this without adequate preparation and I find that it often leads to disastrous results.

Of course, if she feels that her present life is even more disastrous, that is for her to judge, but someone like me cannot estimate that.

Assure her that whatever she decides, I will support her attempts to either maintain the life she now has or build a new one. But I must not become involved in the decision, for that is hers alone to make. And as to lending her the $5,000 to enable her to make it, that is totally out of the question.

Sincerely,

Jim Michener

I still can't understand Jim's response, especially considering his own two divorces and the fact that he had had no qualms about lending our friend William Viterelli money and providing a substantial part of his daughter's tuition at the George School when Vit needed help. Ann calls his response "an ugly, ugly letter," and I have to agree with her. Eventually, "Barbara" did get a divorce, and she continued to work for Jim, as well as taking on two other jobs to make ends meet. But her feelings toward Jim were never the same, and two years later she quit, saying that she found it demoralizing to be struggling financially while working for "the top writer in the U.S."

Jim's fear about being taken advantage of financially was reflected in the way he prepared his estate. One incident had a very strong effect on him. As Jim related it to Ann and me, he had a conversation with Pearl Buck in a limousine on the way to Vineland, New Jersey, where Pearl Buck's daughter stayed in a special school. Jim was to be guest speaker at the school's annual fund-raising dinner.

During the drive, Pearl Buck told Jim that she had been befriended by two dance instructors at an Arthur Murray Dance Studio where she was taking lessons. Her friendship with these dance instructors grew, and eventually she named them beneficiaries in her will.

Jim asked us what we thought about this situation. My answer was that, apparently, Pearl Buck was very lonely, and she appreciated these men who made her life more enjoyable during her last years. If she wanted to leave everything to them, that was okay with me—it was her money. (When Pearl Buck died, the two men did inherit a substantial amount of money and property, but the will was contested by her children, and I understand that a settlement was made.)

Jim was afraid that what happened to Pearl Buck might happen to Mari after his death—that in her loneliness, she might be caught up by the equivalent of a couple of dance instructors.

He was also influenced by the fate of his literary agent of thirty-five years, Helen Strauss. Jim and Mari were living in St. Petersburg, Florida, and Ann and I were taking a drive with them one day when Jim said, "I've been told that Helen Strauss is in dire straits. She made a lot of money from me, and it's all gone. She's broke. And now her company has gotten in touch with me and asked if I would contribute to the cost of her going to a nursing home—to the tune of $35,000 a year."

Jim couldn't understand why he had been approached to help with her support. He didn't feel he owed her anything beyond the commissions she had been paid during their long association.

I know this situation affected Jim's estate planning; he said as much in a three-page, single-spaced letter written in Brunswick on September 16, 1991, to me and three other advisors he had chosen to help Mari manage her affairs after his death (which he assumed would occur long before Mari's).

I have been worried about the frequent challenges to wills mounted by people "who come out of the woodwork," and I am aware that I might be unusually vulnerable since my marriage to Mari, when performed, was illegal in eleven states; and since many Micheners lay claim to a blood relationship with me. Mari might suffer as a result of successful challenges by such persons. . . .

Most relevant of all, I was both shocked and agonized by the misfortune that befell my one-time agent, Helen Strauss. She had been in succession America's premier literary agent, a high official in a Hollywood studio, head of the cinema department at Reader's Digest, and a literary consultant. In these positions she earned huge salaries. I had lost touch with her, had seen her only casually for many years, but when she was eighty, I received this phone call from her accountant: "Your agent, Helen Strauss, has only $24,000 left, which will be exhausted within the next few weeks since she lives part time in her expensive apartment, and part time in a top-flight nursing-care unit. She assures me that you promised some years ago to take care of her for as long as she lived, and we need to know what your plans are."

I was staggered, for I could recall no such promise, except that at the time of her parents' deaths I was as helpful as I could be. Aware that scandal could erupt if it was learned that this brilliant woman was forced to rely upon public welfare, I felt driven to establish for her benefit a fund of $250,000 to be administered by a committee of writers who look after indigent literary people. My only stipulation was that she must stop this constant shifting from her apartment to her nursing home, settle in one place, and live within the means provided by interest from the fund. This arrangement promised to work well, and shortly thereafter she died in relative peace and decency. (The $250,000 was passed along to the writers' emergency fund.) No husband would want his wife to end her days in such humiliation.

What happened to Miss Strauss's considerable savings no one seems to know, primarily because she had no living relative or trusted friend to safeguard her interests. But the money did vanish. Her last days were eased by the remarkable services provided by her successor as my agent: Owen Laster, of William Morris, who, like me, had no obligation to step forward but who did, whole-heartedly.

Even though Jim might not have been aware of his own day-to-day expenses, he kept an eye on the big picture. He had once told me, "You know, Herman, I made almost as much money in investments in the stock market as I made from my books." He intended to make sure that his fortune would end up first in Mari's hands and then be given to the institutions the two of them chose together.

In that same 1991 letter—addressed to me, banker Bill Nash, his lawyer, Bill O'Donnell, and his New York accountant, Alan Wallin—he asked the four of us to serve as Mari's investment advisors. Jim was 84, and he warned us that Mari could outlive not only him, but all of us:

> The women in her family seem to live a long time, so she might be functioning in high gear after you have departed, and this too should be taken into consideration in helping her arrange her affairs. . . .
>
> As a consequence of such considerations, I have done two things: (1) given my wife, Mari, her half of all my earnings, and (2) either given or taken legal steps to pledge the other half of my present holdings to educational and charitable entities which have already been identified but not publicized. These two steps, taken together, mean that I will have only such diminished funds as come to me from now on, while Mari will have control of substantial ones. The purpose of this letter is to enlist the help of you four men to see that she does not fall prey to the disaster that befell Helen Strauss. . . .
>
> Assisted by such a team, Mari ought to be able to protect her future, conserve her inheritance, and live securely and decently. During the last twenty years I have done what I could to educate her in the management of money and believe that she is both knowledgeable and prudent, but everyone can profit from counsel.

The final step in this process took place a year later, in Maine.

Ann and I were looking forward to a short vacation with Jim and Mari in the summer of 1992. The two of us loved the city of Quebec, but the globe-trotting Micheners had never been anywhere in Canada except for Vancouver, British Columbia. Ann and I planned to drive up to Maine, stay a day or two at Jim and Mari's, then motor up to Quebec and give them a two-day, two-night tour of one of our favorite cities.

On our previous visits, Ann and I always stayed at the Chateau Frontenac, so I phoned to make reservations. In Canadian dollars, the rate was $115 a night for a double; that amounted to $85 a night in American money. I thought it was a very good deal. Not Mari Michener! When I told her the cost, she immediately asked, "Did you ask for a senior citizen discount?" I hadn't even thought of it.

"Jim would want that," she told me. So I put in another call to the hotel and, sure enough, we got a 15 percent senior citizen discount, bringing the cost down to $70 a night.

That trip was one of the best times the four of us ever spent together. We strolled along the edge of the St. Lawrence River, where artists were painting and drawing and selling their works, small bands were making music, and outdoor eating places were bustling with activity. We took a bus tour and learned how the city had worked with developers to convert abandoned factories into condominiums and loft apartments. We had a long conversation with the bus driver about the merits of the Canadian health care system.

As we drove the scenic back roads along the St. Lawrence River to Montreal, the conversation turned to the inequality of the judicial system within the United States; for example, in Texas, a person could receive a stiff sentence for possession of a couple of marijuana cigarettes, while in New York the same crime would be penalized by a slap on the wrist. (It was during this conversation that Jim startled us by saying he'd like to have dinner with Jean Harris.)

We arrived in Montreal while there was still enough light to have a good look around, but Montreal wasn't as exciting for us as Quebec. We spent one night there before driving back to Brunswick.

Once there, Jim asked us to stick around a little longer. He called a real estate agent whose office was down the street, to see if he could have some papers notarized. The agent agreed, so Ann and I drove Jim over, where Jim produced a folder of papers.

"You three are going to witness my will, and certify I'm of sound mind and body,"he said. (I couldn't let that pass; I told Jim I'd be glad to witness his will, but couldn't testify to his soundness of mind!)

Once the paperwork was done, Jim said, "That's it. I've set aside $20 million for Mari and donated the rest of everything I own to all the various organizations and charities that I favor. There's going to be nothing left for anybody to claim.

"When I die, nobody's going to come out of the wood-work and say they're a cousin of mine, an uncle, or a brother. I don't want to happen to me what happened to Howard Hughes. The lawyers made fortunes fighting all the claims of people who said they were entitled to a part of the estate. I'm going to die completely broke. Nobody will be able to get a nickel out of my estate."

Frugal to the last detail—even while giving away millions of dollars, Jim didn't want to waste a dime of his fortune on lawyers.

12. The Million-Dollar Misunderstanding

*E*ven when Jim was very young, art was important to him. As a kid growing up in Doylestown, he had a collection of postcards depicting famous works of art which he used to study. Of course, he eventually became so knowledgeable about art that he collected paintings and prints that were exhibited for others to enjoy.

Art was important to me, too, as a boy. I grew up in Philadelphia, about three miles from the Philadelphia Museum of Art, and every weekend, my friends and I would go there for entertainment. We'd spend a couple of hours wandering through the place, up and down its huge marble staircase, and in and out of room after room of great space. Afterward, we'd walk down the Benjamin Franklin Parkway to the Rodin Museum, a small museum which usually was almost deserted, except for its collection of impressive sculptures. If we still had time after that, we'd head over to explore the Academy of Natural Sciences, which was also nearby. It was a great way for a couple of boys to spend the day having fun without getting in trouble.

As adults, Jim and I both had the feeling that public art is important, and that shared interest formed a basis for what I consider to be the greatest result of our friendship, and one of the major accomplishments of both my life and Jim's: The James A. Michener Art Museum in Doylestown, often referred to simply as "The Michener."

Building it nearly destroyed our friendship.

The arts always played a significant role in Bucks County. Outside Pennsylvania, the region was probably best known for the New York theater crowd who spent summers and weekends in their old stone farmhouses. But before they came along, in the first half of the century New Hope was the center of an important colony of artists who painted the beautiful wooded hills, waterways, and emerging small towns along the Delaware River. Some of the better-known names in this so-called "New Hope School" include Walter Baum, Fern Coppedge, Elsie Driggs, Daniel Garber, Edward Redfield, Walter Schofield, and Robert Spencer. But even after their era had passed, Bucks County continued to attract artists.

What we didn't have in Doylestown, the county seat, was any art center or museum.

A group of us, art lovers and artists, tried to raise money in the early 1960s for a Bucks County Arts Center. Ann and I contributed what we could, which wasn't much at the time, and Jim gave $2,000 or $3,000—probably more than anyone else. But nothing came of the effort, and the money drained away to cover small expenses. Jim never forgot that episode, often reminding me over the years of the time he donated money that just drifted away.

But the idea didn't fade away entirely; in the 1970s, when

he and Mari were actively collecting contemporary art, Jim said that he would eventually donate his paintings to the county if we could build a museum to house the collection. A few of us appealed to the county commissioners, and they estimated the cost of a museum at close to a million dollars. Unfortunately, at that time no public official was willing to spend that much public money on an art center.

Then, in the early 1980s, we elected an artist, Denver Lindley, to the county commission. He and another commissioner, Joseph A. Catania, managed to push through approval of a Bucks County Arts Council, with an eight-member board, including myself. We had no budget, but we didn't let that stop us.

To raise awareness of the arts, we came up with the idea of appointing a Bucks County Poet Laureate each year, and we created the Art Mobile, a traveling exhibit hitched to a truck and hauled from school to school throughout the county to teach youngsters about painting and sculpture and other forms of art.

We didn't give up on the idea of an art museum. And in 1985, a grand opportunity came along.

The county had just built a new library in Doylestown adjacent to the 100-year-old Bucks County Prison at 138 South Pine Street. Most of the prison had been torn down, except for the original prison processing center, a forty- by forty-foot stone structure with walls twenty-five feet high, huge turrets, and a magnificent entryway. The location was fantastic; not only was it next to the library, but it stood across the street from the Mercer Museum, a unique poured-concrete structure built in the form of a castle by Doylestown native Henry Chapman Mercer. He had built his museum to house his vast collection of the tools and belongings of pioneers who settled the county—everything from plows and fishing boats to spinning wheels and apothecary jars.

The county commissioners were debating what to do with the property that once housed the old jail, and thanks to County Commissioners Carl F. Fonash, Lucille M. Trench, and Andrew L.Warren, the Arts Council was given a long-term lease on the property and a mandate to turn it into an art museum. Trench suggested we name it after Jim, and she asked me to call him for permission.

Jim was based at Sheldon Jackson College in Sitka, Alaska, at the time. When I told him what we wanted, he hesitated:

"What's it going to cost me?" he asked.

I assured him that his only contribution would be the use of his name, so he agreed.

Converting and expanding the old prison was going to cost. The county commissioners agreed to kick in $400,000; the arts council soon persuaded them to increase that figure to $600,000, and we raised the rest from other sources. The county also appropriated $50,000 to help us meet the art center's operating costs during construction. Of course, that $50,000 was peanuts compared to what we needed.

One winter day soon afterward, while Ann and I were visiting Jim and Mari in Florida, the four of us went for a drive.

"How about making some money for the museum?" I said to him.

"What did you have in mind?" he asked.

"Why don't we have a Bucks County artist paint a Bucks County subject and publish 1,000 prints? You and the artist sign them. We'll call it 'Painting to Celebrate the Opening of the James A. Michener Arts Center' and get $100 each for them."

Mari piped up: "No way is Jim going to sign 1,000 prints."

Our discussion went back and forth. I bargained for 500 prints, and Mari and Jim finally agreed that he would sign 300. I got going right away on the arrangements.

At the request of George Knight, the owner of the Primrose Press, which was located nearby in Solebury, artist George Keating created a fine painting of a Bucks County scene. The scene pictured the manor house of a farm called Blueberry Hill on the main highway through Doylestown, Route 611. Unbeknownst to any of us, Jim was very familiar with that house, and when he saw the painting, he was quite taken aback.

"My God! I used to look at that house every day when I was staying with my aunt at the poorhouse!" he said. "It was just across the road!"

When the prints were ready, George Keating and I flew to Florida, where Jim was at work on *Caribbean*. Mari was in Hawaii, but Jim's literary assistant, John Kings, was there and we set up an assembly line. One of us handed Jim a print; he signed it, then passed it to the artist. George signed, then another of us packed the print into a container—just as we'd worked to stock Joe Kenney's bookstore with autographed copies of *Chesapeake* a few years earlier.

The prints turned out to be a wonderful way to raise funds. Primrose Press paid $100 for each one, and there were an additional fifteen artist's proofs which we sold for $300 each. The $34,500 added substantially to the seed money the county had given us to start the museum.

Then we persuaded a foundry to cast 100 keys, and we

promised one to anyone who pledged $100 a year to the museum for five years, so that we would have $50,000 to cover start-up expenses. Those keys sold out right away; I know people who still have theirs.

At the same time, of course, we were also looking toward the day when the museum would open, when we would need funds both for operations and acquisitions. Our goal was to get the place on a firm financial footing, so that the board wouldn't have to scramble for operating funds every year—or, worse, go into debt to cover costs.

The groundbreaking for the museum was scheduled for September, 1987, and Jim and Mari were planning to attend. Without putting on too much pressure, I encouraged Jim and Mari to make a cash donation and also to donate paintings from their collection to the museum, which we had begun to call The Michener. We also asked permission to create an endowment fund in Mari's name.

Our exchange of letters over a period of several months shows that Jim and Mari had warmed to the project:

> University of Miami
> Department of English
> Coral Gables, Florida
> 15 June 1987

Dear Herman,

Mari and I appreciate your instructive letters. They tell us much that we ought to know, so don't hesitate.

I'm aware that I owe you answers to several questions you've posed, so here goes.

1. Mari will whole-heartedly permit the J.A.M.A.C. to use her name as it deems proper in collecting funds.

2. She will make a substantial cash contribution to the fund, and at the appropriate time this could be announced if that seemed helpful.

3. You can use on a temporary but extended loan basis any of the art work on the hill for your opening show at the museum.

4. Mari will <u>not</u> give the works by the major American painters to the museum permanently.

5. I <u>will</u> give the works [owned] by me permanently to the museum, but the time of giving must be left to Mari.

6. Mari will <u>not</u> give the additional acreage to the college at this time, but I would expect her to do so at some future time.

7. I will not as a matter of deeply-felt principle make any cash gifts to the museum named after me, but I judge that Mari might when it comes time to write her will.

And we both hope that your work on the museum and on the future of your college goes well. You and Annie make a real contribution to your community.

Warmly,

Jim

On August 31, I wrote back with a progress report, ending—as these things often do—with a request for money:

Now we come to the hard part—fund raising.

After much discussion, we have come to the conclu-
sion we don't want to be spending our energies
scratching each year for funds.

In order to make the James A. Michener Arts Center a vital, exciting and important part of the County,
we decided to raise money for the Mari Michener
Endowment Fund. We believe we should try to put
into the Mari Michener Endowment Fund $1,000,000
which would give us approximately $100,000 a year.
With these funds we can hold exhibits, performances,
classes, and other exciting projects which will help
make the James A. Michener Arts Center nationally
known.

We have a large vision for the James A. Michener
Arts Center. We want the center to grow to be alive
and vital for all future generations to enjoy. We want
to do in 5 years what it took the Mercer Museum 50
years to accomplish.

The board of the arts center had decided to establish a
challenge fund at the suggestion of Kenneth W. and Helen
M. Gemmill, well-known community leaders. Ken was a
retired lawyer, and he and Helen agreed to help lead the
fund drive. I hoped that Jim and Mari would make the first
contribution—and I hoped it would be spectacular:

Both of you have indicated that Mari would give
a substantial contribution to the "Mari Michener
Endowment Fund." Could Mari think of giving
$500,000 as a Challenge for us to match with another

$500,000? Her generous commitment would be the stimulus for everyone in the community to realize the dedication you have for this great effort. The excitement of Mari contributing $500,000 to her endowment fund and the publicity that would result would give this fund raising campaign a tremendous boost. This could be given in one lump sum or pledged over a period of several years. . . .

P.S. If you would do this, Ann and I would be the first to pledge $50,000.

We didn't get the half-million I was hoping for, but Mari made a contribution of $50,000, and her gift, together with gifts from members of the board and proceeds from the sale of the prints, gave the museum a good start of $200,000.

The three-day grand opening of the James A. Michener Arts Center, in September, 1988, couldn't have been better. Pennsylvania Governor Bob Casey spoke at the opening ceremonies, praising the attractions of Bucks County. CBS correspondent Charles Kuralt sent an advance crew of five technicians and reporters, and featured The Michener in a twenty-minute arts piece on CBS *Sunday Morning*. And, of course, Jim and Mari were there—they stayed with us, rather than reopening their own house.

Pine Street was blocked off for the big opening on Sunday. We erected a huge tent outside the museum, and the local radio station, WBUX, hosted a dinner party for members of the new museum.

In his own speech, Jim was as modest as always. "When I was growing up," he said, "folks always warned me,

'Michener, if you don't mend your ways, you'll wind up in the county jail.' I guess they were right, because here I am."

So many people came there that day to see Jim. He was great—very generous with his time, speaking to everyone, signing books.

When he walked into the museum for the first time, Jim was impressed. He couldn't get over what we had accomplished with the little money we had. The old prisoner- processing center had been transformed into a gallery, thanks to the generosity of two patrons, Robert L. and Joyce Byers. We also had added a new structure for the main gallery space; with the financial support of the board of directors and much community support, the architect had been able to design a first-class gallery to complement the old stone prison building. Jim wasn't yet entirely convinced that we weren't just a bunch of idealists with a dream that had no staying power, but he had to admit that the museum was a beautifully designed addition to the community.

After all the bustle of the various opening events, Jim was ready for a relaxing drive through the country on the back roads.

"You people have done a wonderful thing," he told me. "It's really quite amazing what you've accomplished with what you had to work with."

He paused. Then he gave me a piece of news.

"It's going to be announced within the next month or two that Mari and I are giving our entire collection of paintings to the University of Texas at Austin. How do you think that's going to affect your ability to raise money?"

This was a big disappointment, of course. And I could see

what he was driving at—people could say, "You have a museum named after Michener, yet he gives all his paintings to Texas. If he doesn't contribute to your museum, why should we?"

I didn't see any point in trying to persuade Jim to change his mind about the gift to the university. But I had an idea.

"Jim, I think if you gave us a $1 million to get this thing rolling, it would make people feel you had a very special interest in it."

He didn't say anything. I didn't know whether he was thinking about the idea, or if he was in shock. Finally, he asked how the donation would be structured and used.

Of course, I hadn't thought about this, but I suggested setting up an endowment fund in Jim's name, with its own board of directors to run it. Jim wanted to know who would be on the board, so I suggested several prominent Doylestown residents: his friend, Ken Gemmill, who had helped lead the fund drive; Earl Jamison, a businessman and a member of the museum's board; and Frank N. Gallagher, a respected lawyer and board member. If Jim wanted, I would also be on the new board.

"Why don't you try to get those people together and let's meet this afternoon at the museum," Jim suggested, just as we arrived back at the house.

Later that day, the group I'd proposed, as well as the museum's director, Linda Buki, assembled at the museum to meet with Jim and Mari. Jim put my idea to them—without much optimism.

"Herman has put me in a very tough spot by asking me to give you $1 million," he said. "My experience has been that small museums like this begin with a lot of enthusiasm by people who think they can make a go of it, then they lose interest and drift away. Problems develop; the museum closes down. I'm not sure I can give you a million dollars because I'm not sure the enterprise will succeed."

Jim didn't have the confidence in us that I thought we deserved, and the meeting ended in disappointment.

That evening, Ann and I hosted a dinner party at our home for the museum board, county commissioners, local dignitaries, and representatives of the governor's office, all of whom had helped us succeed in establishing the museum. At one point during the evening, I noticed Ken Gemmill and Jim walk into my den and close the door.

About thirty minutes later, they came out and Ken told me, "We've got $1 million for an endowment fund, and Jim is very specific about what he wants the money to be used for—operating expenses only, and not to buy art. I'll write up the trust documents."

This was exciting news. In just a few short years, the Bucks County Council on the Arts had managed—with the help of a lot of community leaders, and with Jim's support—to create a fantastic art museum for coming generations to enjoy. There was a lot of work ahead to ensure the museum's financial future, but we had already accomplished a major part of our goal.

A few days after the opening, when all the excitement had died down, and Jim and Mari were back in Coral Gables, I called Jim—I can't remember what for, maybe to make arrangements to see them when we arrived at our condo in Palm Beach after Thanksgiving. I hadn't gotten more than a few words out of my mouth when Jim hung up on me.

"Must be a bad connection," I thought to myself, and called back. To my shock, he hung up again.

Something was terribly wrong. Jim and I never argued, except over politics. It wasn't like him to show a temper, let alone hang up the phone without a word. I called Jim's literary assistant, John Kings.

"John, what is wrong with Jim?" I asked. "Why is he hanging up on me?"

"Jim's very upset and very angry with you," John replied.

"Why? What's the matter?" I was mystified.

"You put him in a spot he doesn't like when you asked him for money for the museum," John told me. "He doesn't like to be asked for money. He feels you embarrassed him in front of other people. He's very perturbed."

I was deeply distressed. Here was a man who had been my friend for over forty years. We'd been business partners and shared a huge financial loss without ever a ripple in our friendship. I was at a loss over what to do.

"Just let it ride a while," John suggested. "He'll get over it."

I let a few days go by, thinking Jim would call. There was no word. I spoke to Mari, briefly; she was cordial, but not encouraging. She, too, said Jim was angry that I had asked him for money for the museum. Finally, on October 17, I wrote Jim and Mari a long letter:

> I have given some thought to Mari's and my conversation concerning Jim's displeasure with me because of his generous gift to the Bucks County Arts. This is puzzling to me because we all have the same objective for the James A. Michener Arts Center.

Jim has said that many museums go out of existence because the people who started them die off and
the next generation does not keep it going financially.
This was and is my greatest challenge to see that this
does not happen. That is the reason I started the Mari
Michener Endowment Fund and will spend my time
making this grow. . . .

[Our] objective, and I am sure it is both of yours,
was to build a facility that would be beautiful and
exciting. The result is we got the old jail plus $600,000
from the Commissioners. It wasn't easy. . . [Our] other
objective was to build a Board of Directors that would
be a credit to the Center. . . . Over a 6 month period
we chose from industry, banking, law, the arts, real
estate and others. This board met each week for a bag
lunch to formulate the policies and objectives of the
Center. . . .

However nothing is more important than building
a strong financial base that will make it possible to
grow and improve the Center. Your contribution will
be something to build on. If Jim feels I pressured him,
I'm sorry. I only suggested to him, in reply to his questions concerning the effect on the Center with his
announcement of his gift to Texas and Hawaii, that a
$1,000,000 contribution would be very helpful. . . .

For the past 15 years, I have [worked] for the arts
in Bucks County . . . I raised $150,000 for an Art
Mobile which was taken to all the county schools to
acquaint young students with the importance of art
in their life. This was my idea, I got the Community

College to manage it, and I got the funds to operate it for 5 years.

I have been a board member of the Pennsylvania Housing Finance Agency for ten years and I have become an expert on low cost housing. I have helped raise over a billion dollars to construct housing for the poor. . . .

I do a lot of things for a lot of causes that in no way benefit me. I'm very public spirited and I generally get results on projects I take over. I don't do it by pressuring people. I do it by suggestion, and if the response is positive, I work out a way to make it happen.

The wonderful gift you both gave has already resulted in the gift of two excellent paintings and more to come. When the gift was announced, Jim became a hero with all the local people who have a respect and love for him. It would be a pity if Jim did not enjoy the results of your generous gifts.

The James A. Michener Arts Center will be here after we are all gone. I want my children and grandchildren to be proud of what I have done here. I know you both want the Arts Center which carries Jim's name to be something that will do honor to you both, now and in the future.

I hoped that when Jim received the letter, he would call me immediately and that we would quickly clear the air between us. But that didn't happen. Weeks went by, and then months. As to his donation, Jim was as good as his word, and within a short time gave the $1 million in two installments.

As we knew it would, the gift generated a lot of publicity and encouraged others to make gifts.

But Ann and I didn't see Jim and Mari when we visited Florida that winter, and we returned to Bucks County without any contact. I tried not to let it bother me, but Ann says that everybody knew it did.

And then, when it was over, it was over. Six months later, Jim called and suggested that Ann and I drive up to Reading to spend the day with him.

"I'm writing a book about the Amish country and I'm going to be spending some time up there," he said.

When we arrived in Reading, he greeted us like the old friends we were. We had a good time touring John O'Hara's old neighborhood in Pottsville, and Jim didn't say a word about the six months of silence that had passed.

Our friendship took up where it had left off.

13. Expanding
"The Michener"

After the opening of the James A. Michener Arts Center, Jim's involvement in the museum grew. Jim was encouraged by the museum's ever-increasing attendance, and by its exhibits, which included not only Bucks County artists but also national and even international artists. The fact that the museum received generous financial support from the county, the state, and from other private donors increased his enthusiasm.

Almost from the beginning, we knew that The Michener would have to be expanded, and we started planning a large addition in 1991, just three years after the opening. We needed $3 million to pay for construction, and I knew I wouldn't be asking Jim for more money!

We got a wonderful start, though, and by June, 1992, with major gifts from Bob and Joyce Byers and other board members, we'd raised $700,000 and felt confident enough to hold a ground-breaking. Jim and Mari attended, and Jim spoke to the 400 people who were crammed outside under a canopy. He told anecdotes about his childhood, and talked about Henry Mercer, who had built two "castles" in Doylestown—

one to live in and the other which he turned into the Mercer Museum across the street.

"How lucky we are," Jim told the crowd, "to live in a town that has not only one castle, but two."

Jim still may have had his doubts about the long-term prospects of the museum, but he couldn't help getting involved. The museum became something he wanted to have a hand in creating and shaping.

The rest of us were concentrating on how to raise the additional $2 million to pay for the expansion, but Jim's mind was on something else—how to fill the place with good art, particularly good Bucks County art.

This time it was Jim who had an idea, and he was willing to back it up.

"What you need to do here is fill this place with art, so I'm going to set up an art challenge," he told us in a lengthy letter. "If you can convince people to contribute forty good paintings of museum quality, from a list of artists I'll designate, I'll add $500,000 to the endowment fund to maintain the museum."

When Jim made a financial contribution, he liked to specify all the details of how it would be spent and even how it would be announced to the public. His challenge grant for art was no exception. In a letter sent from Brunswick on June 13, 1992, he outlined his plan to "tease" some good paintings into The Michener:

> The Byers Gallery is so handsome and so well sit-
> uated that it really must have on its walls choice
> examples of the best work of the artists who made our

district nationally famous in their heyday. When I walked through the Byers this week it seemed to me that it had on its walls only about three paintings that actually belong to us. Someone had done a masterful job of borrowing wisely from other sources, but that is not the posture we should be in. Maintain amicable relationships with people who have fine canvases or sculptures, but now let's make a major effort to acquire our own works, either as outright gifts or long-term permanent loans. We should not worry about who retains specific ownership so long as we have custodial care and assured access. But we must bring the works into our care, so that they can be assured protection and be available through the years. Specifically, I would like to see us have three or four choice canvases by each of our major area artists. Then we could mount terrific shows which would bring our area much favorable attention. . . .

To speed the process, I am holding in reserve half a million dollars to be turned over to the Museum under unusual circumstances. . . . Whenever an art lover from whatever part of the nation gives a museum-quality work by one of our Bucks County or regional artists, the Museum will calculate, in friendly discussion with the owner, what a reasonable evalua-tion might be and, at the moment of gift, my accountant in New York will release that number of dollars from my reserve and hand it over to the Museum. Nothing will make me happier than to be required to turn loose the entire half million, and I

would be overjoyed if that could be completed by this
time next year. The money is there and waiting for
activity on your part. . . .

Jim's letter included a list of about two dozen Bucks
County artists whom he and the museum's new director,
Bruce Katsiff, wanted to add to the museum's collection.

> For example, in the 1920s and 30s, the New Hope
> painter M. Elizabeth Price did a series of large, elegant
> panels composed of motifs from natural flowers, limbs
> and sometimes fruits against gorgeous silver and gold
> backgrounds. In utilizing such themes she was as
> competent as the famous Renaissance painter Carlo
> Crivelli of Venice and achieved comparable results.
> We really ought to have a pair of those panels.

Jim's challenge was a great success. People called from as
far away as Washington State to tell us they had a work by
one of the artists on Jim's wish list, and we got the forty
paintings he had aimed for.

One of The Michener's most important works came to the
museum as a result of Jim's challenge. One of Bucks County's
finest artists, Daniel Garber, was among six Pennsylvania
artists commissioned to paint a mural for the nation's 1926
Sesquicentennial Exposition in Philadelphia. Garber created
a stunning landscape, twelve feet high by twenty-two feet
wide, a dreamy fantasy of water, woods, and deer. After the
exposition, the painting was donated to Mont Alto College in
Mount Alto, Pennsylvania. The school was so small, and the

painting so big, there was only one place on campus where it fit—as a backdrop to the college's stage. When the college librarian read about Jim's challenge, she suggested that the museum might be able to obtain the Garber mural.

Coincidentally, Garber's granddaughter, Dana Applestein, was a member of The Michener's board, so she and a delegation from the museum visited the college to see the mural. After nearly seventy years as a stage backdrop, the mural was in terrible shape and badly in need of rescue. Another board member, Dianne L. Semingson, was married to Pennsylvania State Senator H. Craig Lewis, who arranged for $50,000 in state preservation money to establish a scholarship in Garber's name at Mont Alto College and another $100,000 to restore the painting. It is now a prized possession of The Michener.

In addition to his challenge grant, Jim had another idea for expanding the museum's collection. Earlier that year, he had written to say that some of his memorabilia, then held in the Texas Ranger Hall of Fame in Waco, Texas, might become available, and he saw an opportunity for The Michener:

Austin, Texas

29 March 1992

Dear Herman,

Briefly, when my novel <u>Texas</u> came out, a millionaire oil and real estate man in Waco, ninety miles north of here, fell in love with it and its author. Already the guiding light of a splendid museum honoring the Texas Rangers, about whom I had written favorably, he conceived the idea of adding a small wing to his existing museum as a tribute to me. And he conned the government of Waco into helping in the funds required.

I assumed it was going to be the size of a very small room with a few books about and was stunned that he was building a first-class exhibition space, completely new, completely state-of-the-art, and about the size of a generous tennis court. It was superb, wonderfully fitted out and most handsome. Also it was too big, but he so enjoyed what he was doing that I helped him fill it with a dazzling display of books, manuscripts, portraits, photographs, art work, etc. It wound up a masterpiece, and we had a dedication worthy of a new wing to the Metropolitan.

It was not really germane to the basic concept of the existing museum—which has his enormously valuable collection of guns—but it did no harm to anyone and was a lot of fun for the man who did it.

As you can anticipate, with his death at eighty-five odd, the city of Waco has begun to wonder why they should inherit responsibility for such a big addition to their museum, and I have heard rumors, unsubstantiated and unsubstantial, that they might be wanting to off-load it to some other community, if they could find one. What the words "off-load" mean I do not know. Texans are canny buzzards when they smell a dime and they may have grandiose expectations. But there's always the possibility that they may simply want to get rid of it and would cooperate with any likely recipient. . . .

What did strike me as I listened to the rumors was that if Waco really did want to shed itself of its huge museum to a writer, your board might want to strike a deal whereby you took it off their hands, carted its pieces into one truck of moderate size, move them all to Doylestown and place them in storage until sometime ten or fifteen years from now when there might be space to utilize them constructively. I do not recommend this. I merely point to its possibility.

But if your board did decide that such a move would cost them little, either in shipping or storage, against the probability of future usage, I would cooperate by adding to the collection some eight or ten major manuscripts of my books with all the appurtenances thereto. I judge they would fill about three standing four-drawer files of a size best suited to accommodate standard 8½ by 11" inch papers. If each drawer holds 27 linear feet of folders, 27 x 12 would be 324 linear feet, and to that I would add a very wide selection of my printed books, perhaps five or six feet of shelf space, possibly more.

As I said in the newspaper article, I would not contribute any money to a building of any kind; that would be immodest and improper, but after I'm gone, Mari might want to. Do not tackle Waco's Texas Ranger museum head on. If you want the stuff, try to get everything for free, including the handsome display cases (world class) which you might otherwise be interested in making a deal for. I would pay for the

truck shipping the things north, in order to see that
they received sensible treatment.

Now you know all I know,

Jim Michener

Eventually, we were able to get this material—free—and
add it to The Michener's collection.

Our drive for $3 million to expand the museum was also
successful. We opened an addition of about 24,000 square
feet in October, 1992, without a dollar in construction debt.
The addition was built with private donations and with a $1
million grant from the state. I'm sure Jim's friendship with
Governor Bob Casey, from Jim's old days in politics, helped
greatly. As a board member of the state's public housing finance agency, I would see Governor Casey myself
from time to time, and I also had lobbied him on behalf of
the museum.

We re-opened over a period of three days, starting with a
Friday evening dinner and reception for 200 of the heavy hit-
ters who had made big donations or who had been
instrumental in the fund drive. Jim wasn't well enough to
travel from Austin to the opening, but he made a beautiful
speech by telephone to congratulate us on the opening:

"You people are to be celebrated," he said. "Mari and I
didn't put a nickel into this wing."

The day the public got their first look, on Sunday, was very
special. We started the ceremonies at the Bucks County
Courthouse up the street and marched to the museum
accompanied by a troop of bagpipers. People lined the
streets and waved and yelled and laughed. The line of people

waiting to get into the museum snaked four abreast down Pine Street for more than two hours. It was almost like a Disney World attraction.

My favorite exhibit in the new wing is the recreation of Jim's study from his house on the hill that he built with money from *Tales of the South Pacific*. Jim had allowed us to literally lift the office out of his house, including his gray manual Olympia typewriter, his desk, his files—even the bookshelves. Visitors can see how Jim typed and cut each page before pasting the paragraphs together until he was satisfied. The old hi-fi system he put together on our long-ago trip to New York is there, too, as well as many of the awards he received, memorabilia from his campaign for Congress, and the photos of Jim—wearing different jackets of mine—taken in front of eight of the Doylestown houses where he lived as a youngster.

Another gallery contains examples of the works of George Nakashima, the Japanese-American furniture-maker who lived and worked in nearby New Hope. The Nakashima family donated all the furnishings in this room, and Nakashima's daughter, Mira Nakashima-Yarnell, personally supervised the installation.

As Jim's enthusiasm for The Michener grew, so did his ambitions for it. When his goals couldn't be accomplished as quickly as he hoped, he became very impatient—even bitter. This made working with him on the third phase of the museum's building program something of an amusement-park thrill ride. As his friend and as president of the museum, I frequently got the front seat in the roller coaster.

Construction on the new addition was still in progress when Jim phoned in August, 1992, and asked me to fly up to Maine with the museum's architect, Lynn Taylor, and the museum's director, Bruce Katsiff. I also brought along the museum's fund-raiser, Gwen Campbell. Jim had another idea he wanted to discuss, and he outlined his plan to the four of us during lunch at a seafood restaurant overlooking the ocean.

"Bucks County has marvelous impressionist painters," he said. "But they're not the ones who made Bucks County famous. People like Oscar Hammerstein II, Moss Hart, Pearl Buck, Budd Schulberg, Dorothy Parker, George S. Kaufman—people known throughout the world for the work they did in theater and literature—they're the ones who put Bucks County on the map.

"If we want to keep their legacy and their fame alive, we should have a Hall of Artists to celebrate the non-painting artists of Bucks County," he said.

Then he added a breathtaking sentence: "I'd like to give you $2 million, one to build it and one to maintain it."

Adding a space in which to remember the famous writers, musicians, and composers of Bucks County would complement the addition we were just finishing to hold regional paintings, and Jim proposed calling this new wing the Hall of the Artist.

"I'm not personally concerned with when the Hall comes into full operation," he said. "But I am vitally concerned that the actual construction be started immediately. If the project isn't well under way by July of 1994, the money will come back to me or my estate."

Shortly afterward, Jim sent a letter outlining his conditions for the gift and a list of eight operating procedures for collecting book manuscripts, play and movie scripts, records, and videos. He wanted someone to write a pamphlet about the county's artistic heydays, and he had definite ideas about how informational display panels should be worded. No one was to be included in the exhibit unless he or she had been dead for at least five years:

"Thus there should be no emphasis whatever on work I've done," he wrote. "Of course, in the panels mentioned above it would be permissible to list a couple of my books and perhaps the big television shows, but I'd reserve *South Pacific* strictly for Hammerstein."

On one point he was absolutely clear: "The deadline for having got the new building firmly on the way is 23 July 1994. I do not even suggest any other deadlines."

That gave us a little less than two years to get the necessary approvals and raise additional funds. Bruce and I got to work immediately, contacting county and borough officials, and their approval was almost immediate. The architect seemed to have a good sense of how the building should look, and we moved as fast as we could with architectural and engineering studies, paid for out of the initial stages of Jim's generous gift.

That autumn, Ann and I celebrated our fiftieth wedding anniversary with a three-week trip to France. When we got back, I turned my attention again to Jim's proposed new wing, just as the newly expanded museum was reopening.

It began to look as though we had moved too quickly to accept Jim's proposal and his deadline. The months of

architectural and engineering and financial studies showed
that the new structure would be too expensive to build and
maintain. Throughout the fall of 1992 and the following winter and spring, we kept Jim informed of these studies as they
developed, and while he appreciated being kept up to date,
he was also wary, as usual, that he would be asked for more
money. If anyone had been thinking along those lines,
those hopes would have been quashed by Jim's letter of
May 20, 1993:

> I actually have no funds of my own at this time.
> Everything has been disposed of, and I am much more
> attentive to Mari than I was a year ago, because she
> holds the purse strings (meaning the bank books and
> the deposit slips). . . .
>
> Therefore I can make no further contributions at
> this time. I have had the feeling, perhaps only a
> wavering suspicion at times, that when I promised to
> underwrite the building of the Hall, that management
> interpreted that as a free ride. Taylor's fee was jumped.
> Expenditures were rushed ahead, and bids for the new
> building came in well over estimate. If I were not
> naturally suspicious where money affairs were con-
> cerned, I would not in recent years have had so much
> to give away. I judge your expenditures to have been
> generous but not excessive to a worrisome degree. . . .

Jim did propose that we use $125,000 which remained
from his art challenge, as well as an additional loan of
$200,000—which he would make after completion of the

building—to close the gap between the construction money on hand and the estimated cost of the building. But the board didn't think that was feasible. Two million dollars, generous as it was, wouldn't cover the cost of building and maintaining a new wing. We had just completed a big expansion, which meant substantially higher operating costs, and we had pledged never to run a deficit.

After hours of discussion, the board reluctantly decided to drop the project.

Now we had a real problem. Jim had already given us $500,000 of the $2 million he'd promised. We'd paid the architect about $100,000, the engineer about $50,000, and we'd spent another $100,000 making electrical and plumbing changes to the existing building to accommodate the proposed new wing. We had spent $250,000 of Jim's money and had nothing to show for it.

It was my job to tell Jim the project had been shelved.

I asked him what he wanted to do about the $500,000 he had already sent, and the remaining $1.5 million he had pledged. To my surprise, he was very gracious:

"You can keep the half-million, Herman. I understand."

I could tell from his voice that he thought we should go ahead with the project, even if it meant building the new wing and not using part of it until we came up with additional operating money. But he didn't push it.

Then he made an even more startling announcement: "I'll send you the rest of the $2 million I was going to donate if you'd gone ahead with the Hall of the Artist. I'm sure you made the right decision."

In a letter to the museum's board of trustees, sent from

Austin on June 23, Jim insisted that he had no qualms about the fate of the proposed hall, and directed that the rest of his gift should be added to The Michener's endowment fund:

> Today, with the additional knowledge of your apprehensions, I feel even more strongly that the proposal for the Hall should be junked immediately and totally. It looks to me like a non-starter, an undertaking that can only produce grief. It should be killed. . . .
>
> I have no longer any interest whatever in the Hall. It was a mistake on my part to bring this matter up when I did. The start-up costs of fees to the architect and adjustments to the present building can be written off as a regrettable loss, but you will have no complaints from me.

As I should have known, that wasn't the end of it.

Jim had never let me forget that the Bucks County Arts Center of the early 1960s had "frittered away" his first donation of a few thousand dollars, and a year after the decision was made to shelve the Hall of Artists, museum director Bruce Katsiff and I received this letter from Jim in Austin, dated July 12, 1994:

> I was bitterly disappointed when your Board, for adequate reasons, decided to kill the Hall of the Artist. I'm sure you did the right thing, but it was painful to see the money I had contributed to the Hall diverted into the Endowment. I gave permission grudgingly, but paid in full and on time.

But that action so embittered me that I have lost any sense of responsibility for the Museum. A very bad taste lingers in my mouth.

However, I cannot, in my position, afford to see a museum bearing my name fail to prosper. I have therefore included the Museum in my will, and you will profit from whatever royalties accrue after my death. I hope they give you assistance.

I wish the Museum continuing prosperity and service to Bucks County, but I am constantly aware of how much stronger it would have been had the writers of the area, that remarkable lot, formed the latter half of the offering.

At some later time, Jim changed his mind—and his will— and left his royalties to his alma mater, Swarthmore College. However, Mari remembered The Michener in her will with a gift of $5 million, and after her death, the Mari Michener Wing was dedicated and opened on October 27, 1996. This addition was designed by Lynn Taylor, and its exhibits were designed by Ralph Appelbaum Associates of New York, which also designed exhibits for the Holocaust Museum in Washington, D.C. This gallery is called "Creative Bucks County" and is dedicated to the writers, musicians, composers, and theater people who made Bucks County famous, just as Jim had envisioned.

As much as Jim protested about being asked for money and insisted that he had no sense of responsibility for the museum, he never lost interest in The Michener or in Doylestown, and he and Mari were very generous. Between the two of them, they donated about $8 million to the museum.

One Saturday in December, 1995, I got a phone call at my condo in Palm Beach from Jim, who was in Austin.

"Herman," he said, "I've sent you a letter and some other letters to be distributed by you. The letter is self-explanatory and is in your Doylestown office now. I want you to bird-dog the instructions in the letter."

It was no use asking Jim for details, and it was no use calling my office, either, since it was Saturday. I had no idea what Jim was up to—was it good news? Bad news? Had Jim gotten mad about something at the museum and decided to withhold the money he'd pledged? Maybe he had some ideas about the Mari Michener Wing, which was under construction. Curiosity got the better of me, and I called John Kings.

John wasn't about to spill the beans:

"I can't tell you, Herman, but I will tell you that it is good news and not bad news."

As soon as my office opened on Monday, I called to ask if a package from Jim had arrived. It had, but it hadn't been opened because it was marked Personal and Confidential.

"Open it and read me the letter," I said.

The news was heart-stopping. Jim was going to be named the nation's Outstanding Philanthropist by the National Society of Fund Raising Executives, and he planned to use the occasion of a gala dinner in California to pledge $1 million each to the Mercer Museum and to the Bucks County Free Library in Doylestown.

Neither the library nor the Mercer Museum had ever received a gift from Jim, and the donations would be enormously important to both institutions, especially the library, whose endowment was only $25,000. Jim asked me to quietly inform officials at the two institutions, and to coordinate the announcement of his gifts.

Here are excerpts of his letters written December 6, 1995, to the library and to the Mercer Museum—both vintage Jim:

> Chairman of the Board
> The Henry C. Mercer Museum
> South Pine Street
> Doylestown, Pa 18901
>
> Dear Sir or Madam:
> Your Museum was of great importance in my education. Jimmy Groff, Eggs Hayman and I used to prowl its various levels, ending always on the top floor with the gallows on which so many local criminals met their doom. While inspecting the structure, we took an oath never to commit an act which would bring us to that fatal trap door on which the prison stood just prior to his being hanged.
> In appreciation for what your Museum meant to me as a boy, I hereby hand you this notarized pledge which states that I will give you the sum of $1,000,000 (one million dollars). The money will be delivered at some future date, and you may not take legal action to force me to pay sooner than my plans dictate. Nor may you heckle me for payment at your convenience. . . .
>
> Sincerely,
> James A. Michener

Chairman of the Board
The Bucks County Free Library
South Pine Street
Doylestown, Pa. 18901

Dear Sir or Madam:

Your Library and its predecessor were of considerable importance to me when I was growing up and in
later years when we were doing research on my novels. Since my wife Mari Michener had been a librarian
in Chicago, she and I wanted to express our appreciation. I am therefore handing you this notarized pledge
which states that I will give you the sum of $1,000,000
(one million dollars). The money will be delivered at
some future date, and you may not take legal action
to force me to pay sooner than my plans dictate.
Nor may you heckle me for payment at your conve-
nience. . . .

                     Sincerely,
                     James A. Michener

The Michener remained very much on Jim's mind.

Earlier that year, during the summer, a financial scandal
had broken in the Philadelphia area when dozens of respected, nonprofit institutions—colleges, museums, libraries,
and churches—discovered they'd been duped by a well-
connected fund-raiser, John Bennett, who had promised
to double any investments they made through his Foundation for New Era Philanthropy. It was a classic pyramid
scheme, a type of fraud known as a Ponzi, and for a while

it worked, but when it collapsed, it made national news.

Bruce Katsiff and I received this tongue-in-cheek letter from Austin dated July 20, 1995:

> I shuddered when the newspapers broke the story of the financial guru who took money from scores of famous people and equally famous cultural institutions, and milked them all in a pro-typical Ponzi scheme. How possibly could that have happened to such intelligent people and to the persons in charge of protecting the investments of great institutions?
>
> And now I really shuddered, because I remembered that you two gentlemen had placed all the endowment of our little museum in the hands of a money manager, and I had the horrible thought: "My God! Did they give our funds to this bozo?" I had a couple of bad days. (And did we lose it all?)
>
> To intensify my fears, I saw with horror that one. . . wonderfully public-spirited gentleman had dropped $50,000 to the impostor, and I wondered: "Haven't any of them ever heard of a Ponzi?". . . .
>
> I would have thought that anyone even remotely involved with money matters would be on the alert for the next Ponzi to come waltzing down the highway, but wherever I've lived, I've read in the papers that the doctors, dentists, lawyers and women with small funds to invest have fallen for the alluring Ponzi.
>
> I breathed again when I learned that our fund had been turned over to a money manager, but one of impeccable moral principles and business judgment.

Thank God!

Herman, please post in the museum office a big sign which says PONZI and be sure your money handlers see it every day.

I'm in good spirits and send you all my warmest best wishes. You've been doing a great job and keep it up.

Throughout all the years that Jim helped the museum, worried about it, and protested his involvement in it, I think that he best expressed his feelings about The Michener in his own memoir, *The World Is My Home*, which he published in 1992:

I decided that I was not available for any more public honors. However, just as I started work on these notes I was informed that my home county, historic Bucks in Pennsylvania, was proposing an action that so delighted me that I could not withhold support. The old jail. . . was about to be converted into an art museum, with a big new public library to be erected close at hand. The museum was already named after Henry Mercer, our town's leading and some say only intellectual; the library was to be named after Pearl Buck, our Nobel Prize winner and humanitarian; and the jail was to be renamed the Michener Art Museum. I had hitherto resisted having buildings named after me, but this gracious invitation I could not turn down, because I delighted in the irony that when I was a troublesome boy in town many had predicted that I would sooner or later wind up in that very jail, and here I was eighty years later doing exactly that.

I would like to be remembered in my hometown as a man who helped convert a jail into an art museum.

14. Final Journeys

*B*y the early 1990s, Jim had become increasingly frail. He'd had heart surgery and a hip replacement, but he tried not to let this slow him down. His main concern was getting his affairs in order so that Mari would have a comfortable life after he died.

He accomplished that objective in the summer of 1992, as he says in this note written in Austin on August 18, several weeks after we had visited a notary public in Maine:

> A frightening illness that struck me last week reminded me of how happy I was that in the preceding two weeks I had finally got my financial life in order. I was tremendously relieved and felt no apprehension about leaving with unfinished details. Fortunately, what seemed like a massive heart attack, which might have proved terrible, was a major attack on my spinal column which produced a most painful pinched nerve but nothing more. I can live with it.

Our excursion to Canada had been so much fun that the four of us planned a similar expedition in the fall of 1993. Ann and I planned to drive up to Maine to join Jim and Mari at the end of their annual sojourn there and then continue with them into Nova Scotia. But they got a better offer!

Mari phoned to say that she and Jim had been invited on a round-the-world cruise, all expenses paid, if Jim would entertain the other passengers on the ship with tales of his adventures. Jim was 86 years old, and Mari was 73, but Jim was a great storyteller, and Mari loved cruises, so our trip to Nova Scotia was postponed indefinitely. Jim and Mari flew to the West Coast, where they settled into their first-class suite and set out across the Pacific.

But by the time they docked in Hong Kong in January, Jim had become deathly ill. He had developed heart trouble, and his body was filling with fluids. As soon as he was stabilized, they flew home to Austin. Jim had to be lifted into a wheelchair to be taken off the plane when they arrived.

At the hospital, doctors discovered that not only did he need a pacemaker to regulate his heart, but also that his kidneys were failing. His only chance of survival was dialysis, and the outlook for his recovery was not good.

To everyone's surprise, Jim rallied. Here's his description of the ordeal:

February 15, 1994

Dear Friend:

Please circulate a xerox of this brief report to anyone to whom it might be helpful or of significance.

The numbers tell the story of recent events.

In mid-January 1994 I discovered that my legs were like oak trees—enormous things and hard as wood. I also found that accumulations of liquid had invaded my stomach and thoracic cavity. The hydraulic effect when I tried to put on my shoes was really quite excruciating.

My Texas doctors checked me into a first-rate hospital which specialized in kidney dialysis, it being obvious to them that my own kidneys could not handle the extraordinary excess of fluid. At that time I weighed 184 pounds. After four weeks of highly-skilled dialysis my legs looked like legs again, my weight dropped to 147 pounds, and I was a new man. This is February 15 and my recovery is slowly affecting, favorably, all parts of my body.

I am told that the dialysis may have to continue three hours a day, three days every week, for the foreseeable future and there is no guarantee that even then I will be spared this onerous weekly responsibility.

I would appreciate it if you would advise me as to whether hospital services in your area, in which I might be living from time to time, provide dialysis treatment.

In the middle of my treatment, when the doctors thought I was asleep, they held a discussion near my bed. My personal doctors were not involved, but the ones present concurred that it was highly unlikely, if not impossible, that I would last till morning. This possibility never entered my mind, nor has it since, even though one of my personal doctors confirmed that mid-flight estimate. I fully expected to recover. I could tell that my brain functioning was as strong as ever, but I had no element of bravado about it. I imagined that if things went well I might be able to write one more good book, but certainly not five or six. It is in that mood that I work these days at rejuvenating, adhere to a strict no-salt diet, feel well, have a reasonable social life, and fully expect to get back to Maine and certainly College Harbor as the healing process permits.

I am awed by the performance of our medical team. They really performed miracles. But I am equally impressed by the fact that now, under this splendid system, Mari and I have four highly-trained health workers employed by the hospital who perform home supervision for people like us. I cannot speak highly enough of those non-doctors and non-registered nurses who perform so many of the necessary health services.

I wish you all well and would enjoy nothing better than being with you in this time of my recuperation.

Sincerely,

James A. Michener

Jim did recover, although his kidneys never fully regained their function, and he remained on dialysis the rest of his life. But a disaster was only months away.

For some time, Mari had been complaining of stomach pains. Finally, she consulted doctors. At first, they suspected a heart condition and hospitalized her for a catherization. But instead of a heart problem, they discovered in early August, 1994, that she was suffering from inoperable abdominal cancer.

Jim had always been so sure that Mari, thirteen years younger than he, would outlive him by a good long while. Now, at age seventy-four, she was facing an uphill battle to live out the year.

Mari began chemotherapy treatments in Houston, and these treatments were very hard on her. After two weeks in the hospital, she went home to Austin. She was scheduled to return to Houston for more treatments, but her doctors told her there was no hope of recovery, so she remained at home.

Ann and I called at least once a week. Mari was a fighter, and she tried to keep up everyone's spirits with her strong sense of humor. One day she told us she had fallen while getting out of bed, and wasn't able to get up. She called out for Jim, but he didn't have the strength to lift her. Finally, he called to a plumber who was outside installing a new sewer line. Mari laughed, telling us how ridiculous it felt to have this burly workman grab her under her arms and hoist her to her feet.

On Friday, September 23, we called for Jim, knowing that Mari was too weak to speak on the phone. Her nurse told us that Jim was out, but then we heard Mari asking, "Who is it?"

"The Silvermans," the nurse told her, apparently prompting Mari to ask for the receiver. Mari's voice was very faint.

"I can't talk much," she said. "I love you."

On Sunday, we called Jim again.

"We're all doing okay," he said. "Mari is resting comfortably. We're not hanging any crepe here."

Hours later, Mari died.

Mari was a person with strong convictions, and all the right ones. When I wrote to Jim later, remembering some of the good times we had shared with him and Mari, I reminded him of some of our adventures together—the pricey dinner at Joe's Restaurant, the picture-taking session in the Everglades when we met the sailor who had joined the Navy because of Jim's book, the wedding anniversary dinner with Walter Cronkite. We had had great times together, and Mari was an important part of them.

After Mari died, Jim continued to keep busy. He wrote regularly, and he kept up with affairs at The Michener.

We talked by phone every Saturday afternoon for a few minutes or half an hour, depending on how well he felt. We talked about everything from politics to the murder trial of O.J. Simpson. Jim was following the trial avidly; he watched for three hours at a stretch during his dialysis treatments, three days a week. "It looks like a Marx Brothers movie," he said at one point in February of 1995. "Everything about it is crazy." The antics of Republican House Speaker Newt Gingrich was another of our favorite topics; we agreed that if Gingrich kept talking, he'd probably self-destruct.

As always, we were also corresponding a lot about the museum. I was still very active in the museum, but Jim was involved to a lesser extent. This had the effect of putting a little distance in our friendship. I told Jim that I thought the intensity of our friendship had waned—I used that word with him. We weren't able to see each other much, and Jim didn't like long phone conversations. I decided to visit him in late February, 1996, a few weeks after he turned eighty-nine.

Getting to Austin from the East Coast is no easy matter; there are no direct flights there from anywhere, in my experience. This time I left from Palm Beach and made connections through Dallas, arriving at Jim's one-story ranch house on Mountain Laurel Lane around 1:30 P.M. John Kings and Susan Dillon, Jim's research assistant, greeted me. Jim, they told me, was in his study.

I was surprised at how well he looked. By then, he'd been on dialysis for two years, which can take a lot out of anyone. Except for the fact that he was using a chair with a lift to help him get up, Jim seemed comfortable.

I had planned to take him out to lunch, but John had arranged to bring in food. Before serving us—I had my lunch on a tray and Jim ate from a plate on his lap—John asked if Jim would want to take a nap after lunch. "No," Jim told him, "I've had enough napping."

After lunch, Jim did catnap, dozing for about an hour in his chair while I read *The New York Times*. When he woke, I suggested that we sit outside. It was a beautiful spring day, so we sat in the garden. Jim managed with the help of a cane.

We talked for two hours, mostly about politics, of course. Jim was concerned about the economy, and worried about the number of people being thrown out of work as companies downsized. We also talked about old times, about Mari, and about our trips together. We went over what was happening at The Michener, and Jim's life in Texas. Even before Mari died, John Kings had taken responsibility for many details, and Jim had a wonderful housekeeper named Freddie. When he introduced her to me, he said, "It's okay to get me mad at you, but don't let *her* get mad at you!"

Jim had just finished writing a new book, *A Century of Sonnets*, and had returned the galley proofs to his editor at Random House the previous day. The book, he hoped, would be out that fall in time for the Christmas season. He was still able to get out and see people, and in fact he wondered if I could stay longer than I'd planned and accompany him to a barbecue the next day at a big ranch about 30 miles from Austin. I would have loved it, but my departure was already set, and Ann was expecting me back in Palm Beach the next afternoon.

Around 4 P.M., John Kings and Susan Dillon rejoined us to take us to a basketball game at the University of Texas. I was still wearing the jeans and windbreaker I'd arrived in; I'd planned to change into decent clothes for dinner, but there hadn't been time, so my jeans were just right for our outing.

We piled into a station wagon driven by a representative of the university who delivered us to the door of the stadium for a championship game between the women's teams of Texas Austin and Texas Tech. We were seated at the edge of the playing floor, right next to the Austin coaches. Jim sat in a wheelchair. I sat next to him, and on his left was Ann Richards, the former governor of Texas. We were treated like royalty. Jim was introduced as a guest of honor and got a big round of applause.

The Austin team won, and by then it was after 7 P.M., and Jim suggested dinner. I was expecting to take him out for fancy French food somewhere in Austin—that's what the four of us usually had done when Ann and I visited while Mari was still alive.

"No, I want Tex-Mex food," Jim said.

We arrived at what looked like an old-fashioned diner. Lucky I was still wearing jeans! We ordered a big pile of Texas ribs, with hot sauce on everything. I'd planned to pick up the bill, but John insisted on paying. I think the per-person cost was something like $6.40.

When we got back to the house, Jim asked me to come inside to visit for a little while longer. We talked again about The Michener and how happy he was with the way it had turned out. I left about 10 P.M.

I was so glad I'd made the trip. We hadn't seen each other for at least a year, and nothing takes the place of a visit. I had the feeling that it was worthwhile for Jim, too. As we said good-bye, he shook my hand and said, "Thanks so much for coming."

I saw Jim once more the following spring, in March, 1997, a few weeks after he turned ninety. The University of Texas had decided to honor him with a birthday party of some 300 people. Of course I was invited, but I decided not to go, since I knew I wouldn't get much time with Jim. Instead, I arranged to go to Austin later to spend the day.

This time I decided to fly through Atlanta rather than Dallas, hoping for an easier trip, but the gigantic Atlanta airport, with its widely separated gates, made the distance seem even longer.

I arrived at Jim's at close to 3 P.M.; John Kings had suggested that I wait until Jim had had lunch and a rest. Jim's housekeeper let me in. Jim was expecting someone, but he seemed to have forgotten who, so he was pleasantly surprised to see me.

In the year since I'd seen him, Jim had physically declined quite a lot. He had once been a robust guy, but now
he couldn't have weighed more than 85 pounds. He was
very weak, and so thin; his legs were about as big around as
my wrist.

He was in his study, sitting in his reclining chair with the
lift. I gathered that he was pretty much confined there. He
spent his days in the chair, writing and eating his meals on a
tray. He also slept there because it was too difficult for him to
be helped out of bed at night if he needed to use the bathroom. In the morning, his housekeeper or another aide
helped him wash up and get dressed, and then settled him
back into the recliner. I thought about all the places in the
world that Jim had been, and all the adventures he'd had, and
I was glad he had a lot to remember while he was sitting
there in Austin.

His mind was sharp. Still an avid basketball fan, he had
turned the TV to a college game and muted the volume while
we talked. He didn't miss a beat of what was going on, not in
our conversation nor in the game.

I filled him in about what was happening at the museum,
and showed him some newspaper articles about the
museum's purchase of an adjacent property known as the
Rufe house. He teased me about the way we'd financed the
purchase by taking a loan from the endowment and paying
interest to the museum instead of the bank.

Jim remembered the Rufe house very well. He told me
that during his boyhood he had passed the house many
times, admiring its architecture with its "widow's walk" at the
top, and he remembered that a young woman named Mary

lived kitty-corner across the street. She was beautiful and smart, and every boy in Jim's high school was madly in love with her. But, he said, her folks wouldn't let her date anyone from Doylestown because they felt no local boy was good enough for her.

"Herman," Jim said, "Do you know because of the fact that she was so sheltered by her family, she never married?"

That afternoon in Austin, Jim and I spent quite a lot of time with a portfolio of photographs and drawings of The Michener which the director had mailed to Jim. Jim had recently made an offer—and then withdrawn it—to give the Michener another $500,000 to buy important paintings. In a subsequent letter to Bruce Katsiff and me, Jim had said that his offer was "totally dead," and then—in the same para-graph—that his offer could possibly be revived. During my visit, Jim and I discussed his proposition, but he told me, "Herman, it would take a miracle to convince me," and I decided to drop the subject for the time being.

I could see that Jim was preoccupied with another museum, this one at the University of Texas. He and Mari had donated their art collection, as well as millions of dollars, toward the $50 million the university needed for its museum. Others had contributed several million dollars more, but the university was still short about $10 million. Jim told me that the president of the university had recently asked to speak with him about the museum.

"Jim, we've got some news we'd like to talk about with you," the president told him. When Jim asked what it was, the president said, "You know we had planned to have your name on this museum building. However, there is a trust in town that is prepared to give us $10 million if we name the building after the president."

"Well, go ahead and grab the money," Jim told him. "I don't need my name on that museum. I already have my name on a museum—it's out in Doylestown."

I had the impression that Jim was insulted, but he was too much of a gentleman to say so. He had given millions to the University of Texas at Austin, and Mari had worked hard to get a museum built to hold some of the 350 paintings they had given to the university—paintings valued at more than $17 million. From the start, the museum was to be named after Jim; and now, for $10 million, the university wanted to change that and name it for someone else. I could see that Jim was mad as hell.

For the University of Texas, it was a costly mistake: As a result, all the money left in Jim's estate, and all royalties that would pour in after his death, went to Swarthmore. But it made me very proud that Jim felt well represented in the world with his name on our little museum in Doylestown.

Jim and I had a lot of laughs that day. We talked about the old times and some of our old friends. We talked about President Clinton and the problems he was having. We talked about the sad state of the Democratic party in Doylestown.

Around 5 P.M., Susan Dillon arrived with some lasagna, fresh fruit, and a nice dessert. She asked Jim if he wanted his dinner on a tray in his chair, but he insisted that she set the dining room table so we could eat there. Together, Susan and I helped Jim out of his chair and into the dining room. With one of us on either side, supporting him by the arms, we were able to help him to the table.

We talked all through dinner and for several hours afterward. Jim told me he'd recently been worried about his ability to pay his taxes; he said he'd thought he had maybe $35,000 to $50,000 in the bank. The big money, he said, wasn't coming in any more. (This reminded me of the old days, when Jim didn't seem to have any idea what he was worth or what things cost.)

This time, he'd gotten in touch with his accountant and told him, "I want a hard number. How much money can I expect to earn this year? What can I expect in income?

"Herman," Jim told me, "the accountant came back and said—to my amazement—that I would have $1.5 million this year. I'm going to give most of it to Swarthmore. I want to be able to give Swarthmore all the money I can."

I didn't remind Jim of the letter he had written a year or two earlier, promising his royalties to The Michener. I was disappointed, but I knew better than to argue with Jim over money. Sure enough, he did leave the bulk of his estate to Swarthmore College, but The Michener was very lucky to have been the beneficiary of Jim and Mari's generosity over the years.

That night, Jim nodded off around 9 P.M. His housekeeper told me that he would probably be asleep for the night, so I drove to my hotel.

The next morning, I caught a flight back to Florida. I knew that I wouldn't see Jim again.

Seven months later, he was gone.

It gives me so much pleasure to think of my fifty-year friendship with Jim.

His boundless curiosity, his great intellect, and his tremendous work ethic gave us more than forty books, that widened our world and reminded us all of how much we have in common with one another. His friendship enriched my own life in many ways, and I'm proud of the tangible result—a marvelous museum named after him. We couldn't have done it without his and Mari's support.

With Jim's death, our friendship also came to an end. What's left is my admiration for Jim. I admire him for the way he started out with nothing and made it in this world, for the adventurous life he led, for his sense of humor, for his generosity, and for the way he conducted himself with honor and integrity through all the years that I knew him.

Through good times and bad, our friendship continued, and while I knew his faults and he knew mine, we never let that knowledge hurt our relationship. I don't think you find many friendships like that in this world.

Now what I have are these good memories.

Index

About the Author

*H*erman Silverman helped found the James A. Michener Art Museum in Doylestown, Pennsylvania, and is Chairman of its Board of Trustees. Early in his career he established the nationally known swimming pool company, Sylvan Pools, and he is now managing partner of Silverman Family Partnerships, Inc., a real estate management and development company.

On Christmas day, 1988, after the Michener Museum's board of trustees voted, without the Silvermans' knowledge, to name the main gallery of the museum The Ann and Herman Silverman Gallery, James Michener wrote to the museum:

> Herman Silverman is one of the outstanding citizens of Bucks County. Loving husband, caring father, reliable taxpayer and member of the correct political party, he sets a high example for the rest of us. He has done so many good things for the county that they can hardly be counted, but I am especially aware that he bull-dogged our community into turning the old jail into a new art museum. What a tremendous accomplishment, and how it will bring beauty and distinction to our community.

Of course, you realize he could not have done all
these things without the help of his wife, Ann.

Herman is also a philosopher. When asked what
he would like to do if he had his life to do over, he
said, "I'd like to live over a good delicatessen."

My wife and I join with his innumerable friends in
Doylestown in paying honor to this fine couple and in
wishing them many more years of accomplishment.

Herman and Ann Silverman live in Doylestown.